# Seven Ways of Looking at Language

# Seven Ways of Looking at Language

Ronald K.S. Macaulay

palgrave
macmillan

First published 2011 by
PALGRAVE MACMILLAN

Palgrave Macmillan in the UK is an imprint of Macmillan Publishers Limited, registered in England, company number 785998, of Houndmills, Basingstoke, Hampshire RG21 6XS.

Palgrave Macmillan in the US is a division of St Martin's Press LLC, 175 Fifth Avenue, New York, NY 10010.

Palgrave Macmillan is the global academic imprint of the above companies and has companies and representatives throughout the world.

Palgrave® and Macmillan® are registered trademarks in the United States, the United Kingdom, Europe and other countries.

ISBN: 978–0–230–27930–8 hardback
ISBN: 978–0–230–27931–5 paperback

This book is printed on paper suitable for recycling and made from fully managed and sustained forest sources. Logging, pulping and manufacturing processes are expected to conform to the environmental regulations of the country of origin.

A catalogue record for this book is available from the British Library.

A catalog record for this book is available from the Library of Congress.

10   9   8   7   6   5   4   3   2   1
20  19  18  17  16  15  14  13  12  11

Printed in China

# Contents

*Contents*

# Figures and Tables

## Figures

## Tables

# Acknowledgments

I am grateful to Tom Leonard for permission to reprint his poem *In the Beginning Was the Word* and to the International Phonetic Association for permission to reproduce the diagrams of vowels and consonants. My thanks also to Peter Ohlin for suggesting the idea and to Sarah Dart, Lee Munroe, and Claudia Strauss for helpful comments. Two anonymous reviewers for the press provided invaluable suggestions for revision of the original manuscript. My gratitude also goes to Kitty van Boxel for her perseverance and encouragement in bringing out the book. Every effort has been made to trace rights holders, but if any have been inadvertently overlooked the publishers would be pleased to make the necessary arrangements at the first opportunity.

# Introduction

There are fashions in all forms of science. Even the successors to today's physicists will be working on different problems from those presented by string theory. Linguistics is the discipline that studies language systematically, though the extent to which it can be called the science of language may be disputed since the notion of science itself is tricky. Whatever the answer may be, linguistics has seen many fashions over the past hundred years. The aim of the present work is not to provide a detailed historical account of these fashions but rather to attempt to give those who have not been studying the subject professionally some idea of the kind of ideas and discoveries that have occupied the attention of linguists in recent decades. In the past fifty years, it has been an exciting and lively field.

In my earlier book, *The Social Art,* I wanted to provide readers who are not familiar with the field of linguistics a broad sweep of the kinds of knowledge about language that linguists have uncovered. I tried to avoid getting involved in the controversies that inevitably arise from different perspectives in any scholarly field, not least because the disagreements often focus on technical details that are difficult to present to readers who have not been trained in the subject or kept up with the ongoing debate.

The present work focuses on the kinds of issues and topics that have been explored and debated (sometimes quite heatedly) by linguists over the past fifty years. Little of this has reached the general reading public, and that little is likely to have been misleading, with tentative hypotheses often presented as established facts. The present book is designed to give such a reader a clearer idea of some of the different approaches that linguists have taken. I also hope to convey some sense of the excitement that many of these ideas have generated.

For the most part, I will use only examples from English to illustrate the claims. This means that a lot of interesting work on other languages will not be covered. There are several reasons for this. One is that, fortunately, a great deal of the focus in American and British linguistics has been on English, so that there are usually suitable examples to cite. Another reason is that some aspects require sophisticated understanding of the language, and it is not easy to make them clear to those unfamiliar with the language. So there are many interesting issues that will not be discussed here, though some of the suggestions on further reading may point the reader in the right direction. I will also often use examples from my own research as I know the context from which they come. As will become obvious, I have done most of my work in Scotland, but the few features that differ from other varieties of English should not present great difficulties.

The first chapter deals with **Language as Meaning** for the obvious reason that language would be nothing without meaning. This is a very complex subject and only a selection of topics can be covered, but I have tried to outline some of the more interesting work that has been done recently.

Universally, language communication takes place by speaking. Chapter 2 looks at **Language as Sound**. New methods of investigating speech have revealed more details about how the human vocal apparatus operates in ways that permit fast and efficient communication.

The third chapter examines **Language as Form**. One of the fundamental aspects of human language is that it is structured. For a variety of reasons, I will concentrate on syntax and not examine morphology and phonology. As might be expected, much of this chapter deals with the impact of Noam Chomsky's ideas on the study of syntactic structure, and I have tried to show how his ideas have developed over time. Some other alternative approaches to syntax are also examined.

Chapter 4, **Language as Communication**, examines how language is actually used to communicate in ordinary situations. Like other aspects of the use of language, conversation is structured and has its own "rules."

In every stratified society (i.e., most societies) there are differences in the ways in which people speak, according to their membership in such social categories as gender, social class, age, ethnicity, and region. Chapter 5, **Language as Identity,** looks at the ways in which language reflects (or causes) differences in social status or role. Such differences have historical origins, as does language in general.

Chapter 6, **Language as History,** looks at how language has changed over a long period of history and how it is possible to form hypotheses about earlier forms of language before there are written records.

Chapter 7, **Language as Symbol,** examines the impact of writing systems on the use of language. Speech is fundamental to human language. Language developed from human beings communicating by vocal means, and speech remains the essential and universal characteristic of language. For the past few thousand years, however, there has been a very effective way of presenting language in a visual form.

The chapters are designed to be read as independent accounts. In some ways, each deals with a separate subfield of the discipline, (linguists tend to concentrate their scholarly efforts on at most two or three of these fields). Consequently, it is not essential to begin with Chapter 1 that deals with technical accounts of meaning, or Chapter 2 that provides a technical account of speech sounds, or Chapter 3 that is in many ways the most difficult for the lay reader to comprehend since it deals with abstract concepts that are likely to be unfamiliar to most readers. Yet there is a reason for placing these three chapters first in the book. They deal with fundamental aspects of language that are taken for granted in the later chapters. On the other hand, it is not necessary to have read the earlier chapters to follow the accounts in the later chapters, so the reader may skip back and forward.

Seven short chapters are obviously inadequate to do justice to all the ideas that have emerged in the study of language, even if one were to restrict the survey to the past fifty years. Every year hundreds if not thousands of books are published on linguistic topics. For anyone with the interest and energy there is enough material in print to occupy at least one adult lifetime. This little book is simply a narrative kind of internet search engine pointing in the direction of interesting topics. Like most search engines, it may provide more frustration than satisfaction, but with a little luck it will point you in the direction of some rewarding sites.

At the end of each chapter, I have provided suggestions for further reading. These are works that I consider to provide useful information but a number of them will not be easy reading. It is, however, not necessary to read the whole book to get some benefit, so you should not be put off by their intimidating appearance. Most academics are expert at giving a rapid assessment of how much of an article or book they want to read. Often the introduction and the conclusion will tell you all you need to know. Cultivate the gentle art of skimming and you will be surprised at how much you can learn in a relatively painless way.

# 1

# Language as Meaning

## The meaning of words

The most important fact about language is that it is a way of communicating meaning. If it did not do that, it would be as irrelevant to most of what human beings do as bird song or the sound of the waves. The latter forms of sound are often pleasing to human ears, but they do not help us to conduct our everyday business. Language does exactly that, and more. But from the fact that language communicates meaning it does not follow that it is easy to say what meaning is. There was a famous book by C.K.Ogden and I.A. Richards entitled *The Meaning of Meaning*, which listed over twenty definitions of the word, but in the end it did not succeed in resolving the problems of how to deal with the question of meaning.

Dictionaries are in the business of providing meanings for words but they struggle to provide a definition of meaning itself. *The American Heritage Dictionary* includes even a quotation from the philosopher Willard van Quine: "Pending a satisfactory explanation of the notion of meaning, linguists in the semantic field are in the situation of not knowing what they are talking about." Despite the absence of "a satisfactory explanation of the notion of meaning," the editors go ahead and provide meanings for almost 100,000 words.

The basic notion of a word was given by Ferdinand de Saussure in his *Course in General Linguistics*. He proposed the model of a sign as linking two parts, the concept and what he called the

1

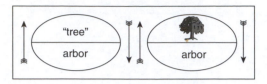

Figure 1.1    Saussure's sound-image diagram

**sound-image.** He provided the diagram shown in (Figure 1.1) to illustrate this notion.

The concept "tree" is linked to the appropriate "sound-image" in a language: in Latin *arbor*, in English *tree*, in French *arbre*, in German *Baum*, and so on. He labeled the sound-image the **signifier** and the concept the **signified**, two expressions that came to be used in a wide range of discourses. The notion seems relatively easy to demonstrate with respect to nouns representing physical objects but it becomes more problematic with abstract concepts, and even more so with adjectives, verbs, and such grammatical words as prepositions. For example, what is the meaning of *of* in such expressions as *the head of the table, a cup of coffee, freedom of expression*?

Even with physical objects, cross-linguistic comparisons show that the notion of "concept" is not a simple one. For example, the English word *river* corresponds to two separate words in French: *fleuve* referring to a river that flows into the sea, and *rivière* for one that flows into another river. On the other hand, the German word *Stuhl* covers both *chair* and *stool* in English. A more complex case can be seen in the range of color adjectives. The color spectrum is a continuum that is divided into different color words in different languages. Some languages make only two or three basic distinctions, whereas others, such as English, may have as many as eleven. Kinship terms also vary greatly from language to language. Danish speakers distinguish grandparents as *farfar* "father's father," *morfar* "mother's father," and so on. Where English speakers make do with a single expression *brother-in-law*, many societies make a number of distinctions in this category of relationship. The entries in a dictionary generally give only the minimum information necessary to distinguish one word from another.

> Dictionaries are like watches; the worst is better than none and the best cannot be expected to go quite true. (Samuel Johnson)

In practice, we seldom bother to consult the dictionary about the meaning of most of the words that we use in speaking. We consult the dictionary only about technical or unfamiliar words when we are unsure of their meaning or in a legal dispute. The original dictionaries were simply lists of "hard words" and designed mainly to help readers spell them correctly. Contemporary dictionaries mostly serve the same function, except for a few readers who are interested in the historical development of the language.

The dictionary maker's challenge is to provide just enough information to enable the reader to make sense of a text in which the word occurs. The dictionary cannot come close to providing all the meaning that the speaker has. (The Spanish Academy reportedly included in its definition of the word for a *dog* that it is the animal that raises one leg to urinate.) For example, the definitions of the word *house* do not include the information that it usually has four walls, at least one door and normally some windows, or that it may be divided into several rooms with different functions, for example, kitchen, bathroom, bedroom. Nor does the definition include the information that for most young people to live in a house it is necessary to obtain a mortgage or pay rent to the owner. Yet these kinds of details are part of our everyday knowledge about houses. When we hear someone say *John and Mary are having difficulty finding a house*, we can immediately envisage a number of scenarios that would fit this statement, but we would not find this information through consulting a dictionary.

The shortcomings of any dictionary are not important for our understanding of human language. The example of the word *house* simply illustrates that we know much more than can be summarized briefly in a dictionary entry. This should be obvious to everyone, but formal linguists (see Chapter 3) often employ lexical items in their models as if their meanings were equivalent to dictionary definitions. They have been able to do so because meaning plays a relatively minor (if any) role in their model. If, however, we are interested in how human beings communicate through language, the wider knowledge that speakers possess about the world is clearly relevant.

There are also what are known as **lexical gaps,** that is, where there is a concept for which we have no single word. For example, the word *bitch* (in its basic meaning) refers to a female dog, but there is no single word for 'male dog,' so speakers often resort to circumlocutions, such as, 'Is that a boy dog?' I used to ask my students to come up with new words for notions that have no single entry in the dictionary. They were often very ingenious in their suggestions.

---

**Some useful words that cannot be found in the dictionary**

*Brashlets* (noun) Those annoying pieces of paper that fall out by the dozens from magazines upon any human contact.

*Misticulate* (verb) To turn a wave into something different upon finding that you don't know that person over there, after all.

*Prantle* (verb) The windmilling of one's arms in a vain attempt to avoid falling or losing one's balance.

*Strett* (verb) To push a crosswalk button repeatedly in hopes that doing so will cause the light to change more quickly.

*Scrimp* (verb) To clean one's room by shoving everything underneath.

*Meanderthal* (noun) An annoying individual moving slowly and aimlessly in front of another individual who is in a hurry.

---

Alas, I no longer have the names of the students to acknowledge them, but they have my thanks if they ever read this.

## Meaning in context

Some linguists would argue that the kind of commonsense knowledge that we bring to the example *John and Mary are having difficulty finding a house* is not part of language, but any speaker of contemporary British or American English would bring such awareness to the understanding of the utterance. It is not necessary to know who John and Mary are or where it is that they cannot find a house. It is, however, often the case that we cannot fully understand an utterance unless we know who said it, when, and possibly where. Charles Fillmore once gave as example of the need for contextual information the message found in a bottle that had floated up on a beach: *Meet me here tomorrow at the same time with a stick this big.* In order to know what this actually means one would have to know who *me* refers to, where *here* is, when it was said, so as to know when *tomorrow* is, at what time the message was written, and what size was indicated by the gesture *this big.* This kind of information is immediately available to the addressee who knows who is speaking, where, when, and can see the gesture, but the finder of the message in the bottle does not have this information. Words such as *I, you, here, now, yesterday,* and *next week* take part of their meaning from who is speaking, where, and when. They are known as **deictic terms**, since they symbolically "point" to aspects of the communication situation. However, we do not need this kind of information to understand the meaning of *John and Mary are having difficulty finding a house.*

---

**Some deictic terms**

| | |
|---|---|
| I | you |
| here | there |
| come | go |
| bring | take |
| today | tomorrow |
| this | that |

---

Many linguists and philosophers who study meaning tend to deal with isolated examples of written language, detached from any context. There are some aspects of meaning that can be studied under these conditions. Some words are classified as synonyms (having the same meaning), for example, *hide* and *conceal*, though they are not always appropriate in the same context (e.g., *John hid in the bushes*). Other words are antonyms (having opposed meanings), for example, *alive* and *dead*. The denial of one of these asserts the other, so that to say *Peter is not dead* is the same as saying that *Peter is alive*. There are other words that have opposing meanings that are not antonyms, for example, *big* and *small*, because denying that something is big does not necessarily mean that it is small. There are also words in a reciprocal relationship, for example, *father of ~ son of,* and *buy from ~ sell to,* so to say that *Peter is Henry's son* is equivalent to saying *Henry is Peter's father,* and if I *bought* something from you, you must have *sold* it to me. There are also verbs with an implied object even when it is not stated. For example, *John is reading* means that John is reading something, though it is not stated what it is. In contrast, *John is sleeping* has no implied object. Other verbs may have an implied instrument, as *Peter kicked the ball.* It would be very odd to say *Peter kicked the ball with his foot,* unless mentioning which foot, as in *Peter kicked the ball with his left foot.* Properties of words such as these can be established from a general understanding of the language and do not require reference to particular contexts of use.

## Meaning and logic

### Analytic vs. synthetic meanings

Some scholars have explored the ways in which logical relationships are encoded in language. One is the syllogism: *All men are mortal*; *Socrates is a man*; therefore *Socrates is mortal.* However, since Plato's day few people conduct their conversations to illustrate such conclusions. Another aspect of meaning that has attracted the attention of philosophers is the notion of necessary truth in contrast to contingent truth. If I say *It is raining outside*, this statement is true if in fact it is raining outside and false otherwise. If, however, I say *All dogs are mammals*, it is not necessary for the hearer to examine any particular dog to find out whether this is true. It is part of the definition of the concept "dog" that it is a mammal. Apparent counter-examples such as china dogs and toy dogs are not considered to affect the truth of the general statement that all dogs are mammals. Expressions that require reference to circumstances in the world are called **synthetic** while those that do not require such validation are **analytic**. Despite the attention they have received from philosophers and some linguists, analytic statements are not common in social interaction, and consequently they are not central to an understanding of how people use language.

## Entailment

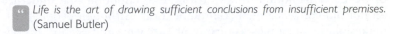

> *Life is the art of drawing sufficient conclusions from insufficient premises.*
> (Samuel Butler)

Some linguists have also been interested in the logician's notion of entailment. This is the notion of what can be deduced from a statement. For example, if I say *I saw a coyote in the street today* and I am speaking accurately then it necessarily follows that I saw an animal. Thus the statement *I saw a coyote* entails 'I saw an animal' but the statement *I saw an animal* does not entail 'I saw a coyote' since there are many other kinds of animals. Similarly, if I say *All the students passed the exam* this entails that some of the students passed the exam (since *all* includes *some*) but *Some of the students passed the exam* does not entail that all of the students passed the exam. The notion of entailment, however, is again of limited interest when looking at how people use language meaningfully, though many examples reveal the complex semantic content of words, as in the example of the coyote being an animal. If I say *I saw a man on the corner today*, this entails I saw something and that the something was an adult human being and also that the human being was male. These are essential features of the word *man*. If I say *I saw a box on the corner today*, it still entails that I saw something but that something is no longer human or male.

Given the importance of lexical items in recent accounts of syntax (see Chapter 3), the semantic features of words are of obvious importance. Entailment is, among other things, one way of identifying these features and determining the truth or falsity of an utterance. It is philosophers rather than linguists who are concerned (some might say obsessed) with whether an expression is true or false. The 19th-century German statesman Metternich is reputed to have said that one of the commonest uses of language is for the concealment of thought. This may be more true of diplomacy than in everyday uses of language but we all know that in many cases what we say is not "the whole truth" and sometimes not even close to it.

## Implicature

> *I'm fond of children (except boys).* (Lewis Carroll)

A more interesting aspect of meaning in relation to communication is what has been called Implicature. This involves looking at what is implied beyond what is stated explicitly by the sequence of words. This notion follows from an assumption that underlies all normal conversational communication. Although people often make jokes, sometimes use irony or sarcasm, and even occasionally tell lies, in everyday conversation we take it for granted that our interlocutor is speaking "in good faith," unless there is any reason to believe otherwise. There are some consequences of this understanding. One is that we expect people to tell us as much as we need to know but not too much more, though both expectations are sometimes unjustified.

For example, if I tell you *Some of the students passed the exam* you would probably be annoyed or at least puzzled to learn later that I knew that all the students had passed. If I knew that they had all passed, why did I only say that some had passed? This is not a matter of lying. When I say *Some of the students passed the exam*, this is true even if all the students passed, but while I am telling the truth I am not telling the whole truth. A parallel situation exists if I say *Not all the students passed the exam* when I know that none of the students passed. Similarly, if I say *I believe that Peter passed the exam*, this would be a very odd way to say it, if I knew for certain that Peter had passed. We expect people to use expressions such as *all*, *none*, and *know* (instead of *some*, *not all*, and *believe*) when these forms more accurately reflect the situation. It is not that we expect people to tell the truth all the time but we do not expect them to mislead us in this kind of way. This is part of a general process of interpretation that takes place in communication, as will be discussed below, but there is another systematic aspect of meaning that must be considered first.

## Presupposition

> An Alford plea is a plea of "guilty" containing a protestation of innocence.
> (Legal definition)

An interesting aspect of meaning is what is called presupposition. If I say *Please shut the door* my request makes it clear that I believe the door to be open, though I have not actually said so (and I may be mistaken). Linguists call the implication of this belief Presupposition. Similarly, if I say *Please do not shut the door* my request still signifies that I believe the door to be open. The change from an affirmative to a negative request does not affect the presupposition. It does not matter whether the door is actually open or closed; the point is that my request implies that I believe the door to be open.

A more complicated example is: when I say *Mary noticed that the door was open* the presupposition in my statement is that the door was open and this presupposition still holds if I say *Mary did not notice that the door was open*. Again, the negative does not affect the presupposition. It is very different if I say *Mary believed that the door was open*. In the latter case, I may (or may not) know whether the door was open or not; my statement about Mary's belief carries no presupposition about my knowledge of the door being open or closed. Note that again my belief may be mistaken. In saying *Mary did not notice that the door was open* I may be mistaken in my belief that the door is open when in fact it is closed, but the presupposition does not depend upon the accuracy of my belief. The notion of presupposition simply means that when I utter a request such as *Please shut the door* in good faith and under normal circumstances, I believe that the door is open. The conditions "in good faith" and "under normal circumstances" exclude situations where I am lying, joking, or using language in some unpredictable way.

Negation can also help to distinguish between entailment and presupposition. If I say *Peter managed to open the box*, this entails that Peter opened the box. It also presupposes that Peter *tried to open the box*, since the expression *managed to* contains the notion of a deliberate attempt to do something. If I say *Peter didn't manage to open the box*, there is no entailment that Peter opened the box, since he obviously did not succeed. However, the presupposition that he *tried* to open the box still holds. On the other hand, it is possible to cancel the presupposition. I can say *Peter didn't manage to open the box – in fact he didn't even try*. This shows that presuppositions, unlike entailments, are not always absolute. Nevertheless, in the absence of an immediate contradiction, the presupposition holds its force. As with implicatures, presuppositions are such a basic part of our communication system that we seldom pay conscious attention to them as such, though we take them into account in our everyday conversation. Their significance may play an important role in legal disputes as to what had been agreed in a contract.

## Meaning in action

In interacting with others in our own community we behave in certain predictable ways and we expect others to behave in a similar fashion. We would be very surprised if someone we know said: *Be so good as to stand up, move ten paces in front of you, take the handle you see in front of you, turn it to the right, and pull it toward you* instead of: *Please open the door.* Depending upon one's relation to the addressee, the same request might be worded as *Would you mind opening the door?* or more abruptly as an order *Open the door!* but a detailed instruction of the different movements involved would only be used in abnormal situations. Generally, speakers express themselves as briefly as possible, as if literally saving their breath. This can be understood as a general principle: speakers do not usually speak at greater length than is necessary to convey the information to the listener. Obviously, there are occasions on which this is not true but adults are likely to feel they are being treated as children (or worse) if the principle is blatantly violated.

There is a complementary principle: normally speakers do not deliberately give less than the information needed for the listener to understand the situation. For example, if you enquire about the number of children Peter and Helen have, it would be misleading for me to reply *They have three daughters* when in fact I know that they also have two sons. What I said was true but, as in the examples given above with *some* and *all*, it was not the whole truth. There may be many circumstances when I do not wish to be totally truthful and will deliberately suppress some information, but in most situations I will reply as accurately as I can and will expect others to do the same. It is this kind of mutual understanding that allows everyday communication to proceed so smoothly and economically. The difference can be seen in legal documents and court proceedings where every inference and implication needs to be spelled out because there is no mutual trust.

This principle accounts for the inference that when you state a weaker claim, you are denying a stronger one. So if I say *some,* it implies *not all*; if I say *I think Peter has red hair,* by using the word *think* I imply that I do not know for certain. If I say *Helen often chairs the meeting*, the use of the word *often* implies that she does not always chair the meeting, and so on. There may be reasons, such as tact or timidity, why I deliberately decide to use the weaker form in certain situations, but otherwise the use of the weaker form denies the stronger. We have a kind of mental scale that runs from *all > most > many > some > few* and from *certain > probable > possible* according to which we interpret any item on the right to deny those that proceed it on the left. So if I say that something is possible, I am making it clear that I do not have any reason to believe it is probable or certain.

## Reference

Central to understanding the meaningfulness of communication is the notion of Reference, or what is being talked about. Earlier in this chapter, the category of deictic elements was mentioned. These are expressions such as *I, you, here, today, last week, the day after tomorrow*. Such expressions take their meaning from the speaker and the time and place of the utterance. Obviously, I use *I* to refer to myself and *you* to refer to the person I am addressing, but the reference of both pronouns changes when my interlocutor replies. Such items are sometimes known as **shifters** because their reference switches with the speaker, whereas expressions such as *here* and *today* may be shared by speaker and addressee. There are also verbs that reflect the orientation of the speaker, as in the difference between *When you come, please bring the packet,* and *When you go, please take the packet.* The verbs *come* and *bring* indicate the direction toward the speaker, while *go* and *take* are used when the direction is away from the speaker.

Deictic expressions are governed by the conditions of Who is speaking to Whom, Where and When, so they cannot be fully understood without examining the context of the utterance. There are other examples of referring expressions that require the speaker to take into account what the addressee knows. For example, if I say *I bought a car yesterday*, I do not expect the listener to know which car. The expression *a car* is **new information**. If, on the other hand, I say *I bought the car yesterday*, I am assuming that the addressee will know which car I am referring to. There is no semantic difference between *I bought the car* and *I bought a car*. In each case, there is a singular object, a car, and the speaker purchased it. The difference lies solely in my belief that the addressee knows or does not know which car I am referring to. This may be a mistaken belief and the addressee may reply *Which car?* or some similar question. The essential point is that in using the expression *the car* the speaker is making an assumption about shared knowledge.

The difference between *the car* and *a car* is the use of the article. The labels for the articles are somewhat misleading. *The* is called the **Definite Article** and *a* the **Indefinite Article,** but the labels do not accurately indicate the difference between them. When I say *I bought a car*, I am referring to a specific object just as clearly as when I say *I bought the car*. The difference, as pointed out above, is in the speaker's understanding of the addressee's shared knowledge. There is no difference in reference between the two sentences because the verb indicates a singular action at some specific (though unstated) time. However, in different contexts there is a possible difference in the use of the articles. For example, if I say *I want to buy a car*, there is an ambiguity. There may be a specific car that I wish to buy, or it may be the case that I simply want to buy some kind of car. In the sentence, *I want to buy the car* there is no such ambiguity, as there must be a specific car I wish to buy.

It is not always the case, however, that the definite article *the* indicates a specific referent. In the proverb *The early bird gets the worm* there is no reference to any specific bird or worm. This use of the definite article is called the **generic** use and occurs most frequently in definitions, such as *The whale is a mammal*. The indefinite article can also be used generically as in *An apple a day keeps the doctor away* or *A beaver builds dams*. There is also an interesting use of the definite article with *same* that does not have the normal referential sense. An example is *Mary and Helen were horrified to find that they were wearing the same dress* where it is unlikely that they were both encased in one garment. The use of the articles in English is highly complex and causes many problems for foreign learners whose languages have different ways of indicating reference. Since the articles are among the most frequent items in both spoken and written communication, it is clear that they present a major challenge for any theory that depends solely on computing meaning from a combination of items.

## Indirect meaning

The process of understanding each other seems so easy and natural that it is sometimes difficult to realize just how complicated the whole process is. We are accustomed to taking into consideration not only the meanings of the words that are used and the constructions in which they occur, but also the context in which the utterance is made and also the tone of voice. In a situation where you have just dropped a cup or a glass and it broke and someone says *That was clever* you know that it is not meant as a compliment. It does not take any special intonation to indicate the intended meaning. Similarly, if you are out in the country for a picnic and it starts to rain heavily, someone can say *What a lovely day for a picnic* without underlining the irony by the tone of voice. Someone may respond to being told to do something by saying *At once, sir ~ yes, mother ~ of course Your Highness* or some other inappropriate form of address to indicate that one is being treated as an inferior, a child, or a subject.

As adults, we seldom have difficulty in detecting sarcasm or irony (though children do not always recognize it). We are able to do so because we have expectations that what people say will be appropriate and meaningful. This allows us to interpret remarks in a way that most computer programs would find difficult. The following example has been cited in many accounts of language interaction.

> Mary: That's the telephone
> Peter: I'm in the bath
> Mary: OK

Mary's remark is clearly intended to ask Peter to pick up the telephone. Peter's reply reveals why he is not in a position to do so, and Mary's response indicates that she accepts this explanation. The explanation of this kind of sequence comes in what has become known as **Speech Act Theory.**

The framework for speech act theory was set by John L. Austin in a series of lectures that were published under the title *How to Do Things with Words*. Austin pointed out that the syntactic form of an utterance does not necessarily indicate its function. In most cases questions are a request for information, but the utterance

*Can you pass me the salt?* is not a question about the addressee's ability to pass the salt but a request for him/her to pass the salt. Similarly, the utterance *Why don't you tell her?* is probably not a question about the addressee's reluctance to tell her but a suggestion that he should tell her. The utterance *It's about to collapse* could either be an observation or a warning. The statement *It was unforgivable* could be a comment on someone else's action or an apology for one's own.

## Illocutionary acts

Austin made an important distinction between what he called a **Locutionary Act** and an **Illocutionary Act,** though the unfortunate similarity in the terminology does not make it easy to remember which is which. By locutionary act, Austin simply meant the act of producing an utterance, so it is not necessary to remember that term. The notion of an illocutionary act, however, is very important. By illocutionary act, Austin meant the rhetorical force of the utterance, the speech act that the utterance exemplified. We use language for many illocutionary acts: requesting, directing, threatening, promising, informing, inquiring, congratulating, advising, thanking, apologizing, welcoming, and so on (Table 1.1). Perhaps Austin's most important point was to emphasize that one form of utterance can perform different illocutionary acts, as in the examples of questions in the previous paragraph, and conversely an illocutionary act can be expressed by a variety of types of utterance. There is thus no one-to-one relationship between the form of an utterance and its function.

Austin also set out the conditions for what he called **Performatives,** for example, naming a ship, performing a marriage ceremony, or making a bet. Utterances of this kind present a problem for semantic analysis because the notions of truth or falsity do not

Table 1.1    Types of illocutionary acts

| Asserting | Requesting | Promising | Apologizing |
|---|---|---|---|
| Predicting | Questioning | Offering | Congratulating |
| Describing | Prohibiting | Baptizing | Thanking |
| Informing | Permitting | Wagering | Greeting |

apply to them, yet there are criteria that make them appropriate or not. For example, you cannot legitimately promise to do something that is impossible. If someone says *I promise to take you to Mars for a weekend next month*, you would not treat it as seriously as an offer of a weekend in Las Vegas. Nor can you make a legitimate promise to obey the law of gravity, since you have no freedom to decide whether to obey it or not. In order for a speech act to be legitimate, there are special conditions that must be met, and Austin and others have tried to specify these.

## Indirect speech acts

There are also cases of indirect speech acts where the speaker does not want to be transparent. For example, instead of asking someone directly for a loan one might say *I don't know how I'm going to pay my rent this month* or in a situation where it is raining hard you might say *Do you have a car?* hoping to be offered a ride. Examples such as these show that it is impossible to set up a theory of meaning in communication based simply on the dictionary meanings of words and their combinations into sentences.

There are also situations in which the surface meaning of the words or expressions may conceal a different intention. The satirical British television program *Yes Minister*, gave some translations of the language of bureaucracy. The statement that something is "under consideration" is a way of saying "we've lost the file," while saying that it is "under active consideration" means "we're trying to find it." The admission "I think we have to be careful" means "we are not going to do this." Responding to some proposal saying "with the greatest possible respect" means "that is the silliest idea I've ever heard of." These examples may exaggerate the distinction between "what is said" and "what is meant", but they illustrate the problems in trying to deal with meaning in actual speech.

## Metaphorical meaning

There are also basic problems with the dictionary meanings of words. We often use words metaphorically, that is, we use them because of their associated meanings (connotations). For example, if I say *John's a brick*, I am saying that John has certain strong qualities that make it easy to depend upon him, but there is nothing in the definition of the word *brick* to indicate this. The usage has become so common, however, that a subsidiary meaning for the word in *The American Heritage Dictionary* is "a splendid fellow." There are many examples of metaphors that have become so established that we hardly think of them as metaphors. George Lakoff and Mark Johnson, in their book *Metaphors We Live by,* list numerous metaphors that have become a stable part of the language. For example, they point out that "happy" is up and "sad" is down: *My spirits rose; he's really low these days.* This extends to health: *he's in top shape; he's sinking fast.* They give an extended illustration of the metaphor of "love as a journey."

Look *how far we've come.*
We'll just have to *go our separate ways.*
I don't think this relationship is *going anywhere.*
We're just *spinning our wheels.*
We've gotten *off the track.*

Sadly, most of their examples indicate journeys that end unhappily. Lakoff and Johnson point out that the notion of "love is a journey: is a reflection of a way of thinking, not simply a matter of combining words, thus it is possible to create new metaphors with the same implication, for example, "our relationship *took a nose-dive.*"

Lakoff and Johnson argue that metaphors are so pervasive in our speech that they reflect cultural values. They list other metaphors for love: Love is a physical force (*They are attracted to each other*), Love is a patient (*Their marriage is on its last* legs), Love is madness (*I'm crazy about her*), Love is magic (*She cast a spell over me*), and Love is war (*He won her hand in marriage*). Such metaphorical uses are so common that it is easy to think of other examples in each category. Metaphors are also common in polemical writing.

Metaphors are also the basis of multiple meanings of words. One of the problems for a dictionary maker is to distinguish between words that sound (or look) the same, but are unrelated to each other (**homonymy**) and words that have a wide range of meanings that can somehow be related to each other (**polysemy**). A common example of a homonym is the form *bank*. There is no connection between the notion of a financial institution and the side of a river. Consequently, there are two words, though they both have the same form *bank*.

Another form of homonymy is what are called "two-way words." When you *dust* crops, you sprinkle the dust on them. When you *dust* the furniture, you remove the dust. Another example is the verb *dry*. There is a children's riddle: "What is it that the more it dries, the wetter it gets?" The answer: A towel. The verb *dry* can either be transitive, that is, take an object, or intransitive, without an object. In the transitive use, the drying affects the object; in the intransitive use, the drying affects the subject. In the riddle, the towel is transitively drying something else, and getting wetter in the process.

Polysemy can be illustrated by the word *head*.

John's head
the head of the committee
the head of the river
the head of a pin
the head of the parade
a head of cabbage
several head of cattle
the head of the tape recorder

*The American Heritage Dictionary* lists twenty-eight different (but related) senses of the word *head*.

The existence of polysemous words is another example of the economical use of language. Instead of having to store twenty-eight different word-forms in our memory, we can interpret the intended meaning from the context in which it is used. Homonymy also allows the possibility of puns: *Toyota Motor Corp is the colossus of roads.* Some people may find this one of the less attractive features of language.

## Polysemy

We also use words with significantly different meanings although the reference is the same, as in the example *This book is a really valuable account of semantics but it weighs three pounds.* The first reference is to the book as a text, that is, what the book is about, but the second reference is to the physical object that contains the text. These are quite distinct meanings but we do not usually have any difficulty in separating them because of the context. In an isolated example if someone says *This is a dirty book*, in most cases the hearer would interpret it as referring to the contents, but there might be circumstances in which the actual copy was in a soiled condition. In the latter case, to refer to it as a *dirty book* would probably be intended as a joke, similar to a pun.

There are other circumstances where we find it easy to understand the underlying meaning. If someone says *A green Mercedes drew up in front of the hotel*, we know that the car itself did not do this. The driver of the Mercedes stopped the car there, but we do not need to be told this specifically. If someone standing in front of you in a room says *I am parked out back,* you know that he is referring to his car, not to his own body. Polysemous words are a major part of our vocabulary but we usually do not need to stop and think which of their meanings is appropriate. The context guides us to make the right choice.

A related aspect of meaning is the use of **idioms**. Idioms are sequences of words that have acquired a meaning in combination that is quite different from normal sense. For example, the expression *blow the whistle* has an idiomatic meaning that is distinct from its literal one. There is no way in which the idiomatic meaning could be constructed from the meanings of its component parts. Many commonly used idioms in English consist of a verb and a particle, as in *I give up, he didn't let on, they headed off,* and *Mary and John have broken up.* In turn, combinations of a verb and a particle can be used with very different meanings, as in the different meanings of *put on* in *put on the television, put on weight*, and *put on your clothes*. Such idiomatic expressions are again very economical in terms of memory storage, but they cause problems for foreign learners of English.

## Formulaic expressions

Similar to idioms are **clichés**, that is, expressions that have been used so frequently that they have become formulaic, for example, *it's a hard life, it takes all kinds,* and *never say die.* Although many fastidious speakers deplore and avoid clichés, they often occur in everyday conversation, especially in situations when it is not easy to decide what to say. Clichés (such as the examples given) can serve a useful purpose in expressing sympathy or support without committing the speaker to specific details. It hardly needs to be pointed out that language can be used in concealing thoughts or attitudes as effectively as in expressing them. Modifying the expectations of a cliché as Samuel Butler does in his aphorism, "The best of friends must meet" is a common form of humor. Mae West in her films often used this kind of device: "I've been things and seen places."

There are also examples of clichés that might seem not to contain any new information and yet they can be used meaningfully. Examples are **tautologies** such as *boys will be boys* and *war is war.* In both cases, the meaning likely to be conveyed is that the addressee should not be surprised at what has happened (or is about to happen). Neither expression could be analyzed to provide this interpretation. A similar practice sometimes can be found in the use of proverbs, for example, *it never rains but what it pours, every cloud has a silver lining,* and *it's always darkest before the dawn.* It is highly unlikely that such expressions are ever used with reference to atmospheric conditions.

There are also many expressions that can be said to have no paraphrasable meaning. They include greetings such as *How are you?, Hello,* and *Hi!* and parting signals such as *Goodbye, So long!* and *Seeya!* These expressions have an important function but little semantic content. There are also many words and expressions that are used regularly in conversation for interactional purposes although they have no fixed meaning. Such expressions are sometimes called **Discourse Markers** and they include *oh, well, you know, I mean, you see* and for many younger speakers *like.* These expressions will be examined in Chapter 4.

## Semantics vs. pragmatics

One of the central issues for linguists in the study of meaning has been where to draw the line between Semantics and Pragmatics. Traditionally, semantics is the part of linguistics dealing (1) with the meaning of words that speakers have stored in their mental lexicon, (2) with the meaning of sentences in which these words are combined, and (3) with what these expressions refer to in the world. Frustration with some of the perennial problems that arise when dealing with meaning in this framework has led to the development of a new division of linguistics. Pragmatics, in contrast to Semantics, examines the general principles of how the context of utterance affects the meaning and how listeners interpret what is said. In recent years, there has been a desire to draw a sharp line between semantics and pragmatics.

Central to this debate have been little words such as *and, but,* and *so*. For example, in the sentence *driving home and drinking three beers is better than drinking three beers and driving home* the inference is that in both cases *and* means "and then," although the dictionary meaning of *and* does not require this interpretation. Similarly, it has been reported that the actress Kathleen Turner turned down a script that called for an actress "37 years old but still attractive" since the implication of *but* is that 37-year-old women are not generally believed to be attractive. In the sentence *he was hungry, so he went to McDonalds*, the implication is that his hunger was the cause of his going to McDonalds. All these examples illustrate problems for an approach based on the dictionary meanings of words such as *and, but,* and *so*, because they require the broader context (and sometimes common knowledge) to convey the meaning of the utterance.

It is probably fair to say that the semanticists have been fighting an uphill battle in recent years. The problem is that any sentence formed by the combination of words underdetermines the meaning of any utterance. Many years ago it was pointed out that the sentence *John is playing golf* could be used to convey more information than the meaning of the combined words. For example, it could be used to indicate that John had recovered from his operation, or to reveal why John had failed to turn up for an important meeting. It is impossible to have a theory of language that will account for all possible meanings that an utterance might have in a particular context, but pragmatists have been attempting to establish a set of general principles that will allow predictions about how a listener can recognize what the speaker intended to communicate.

## Generalized vs. conversational implicatures

One issue has been whether it is possible to distinguish two different kinds of implicature. It has been suggested that there is a difference between **Generalized Conversational Implicatures**, which apply without taking the immediate context into consideration, and **Particularized Conversational Implicatures**, which apply only in a specific context. An example of the first kind of implicature is the utterance *Mary caused the car to stop* which implicates that she did so in some less predictable manner than if the speaker had said *Mary stopped the car*. The example of *John is playing golf* with the implicature that he has recovered from his operation would be an example of a Particularized Conversational Implicature, dependent upon the speaker's and listener's knowledge of the situation.

## Relevance theory

No distinction of this kind is made in what has been called Relevance Theory. This theory states that all utterances are assumed to be relevant in the specific context and, therefore, the listener should expect to be able to understand what the speaker intends. At the same time, it holds that the linguistic meaning alone is not sufficient to reveal what the speaker has in mind. The theory asserts that the utterance should be as easy as possible for the listener to understand and also that it should contain some information of interest to the listener. Finally, the theory claims that listeners in ordinary forms of interaction will make little effort to examine the utterance for subtle ambiguities. Rather, they will stop processing the signal when they have reached an appropriate interpretation. According to this theory, speakers are expected to make their utterances relevant and listeners are expected to respond by treating the utterance as relevant. Only when there seems to be something inappropriate with the message (e.g., in sarcasm) will the listener seek another meaning. Relevance Theory is an attempt to bring together many of the notions about the pragmatic interpretations of meaning that have been presented above, but it has not been adopted by all pragmatists.

## Sentences vs. utterances

It is possible to draw a sharp distinction between semantics and pragmatics by distinguishing between "**sentences**" and "**utterances**." Syntacticians are concerned with sentence structure (see Chapter 3). English sentences often consist of a subject, for example, *the little boy*, a verb of some sort, for example, *was rolling*, an object, for example, *a ball*, and sometimes an adverbial expression of some sort, for example, *along the grass*. Syntacticians have concerned themselves with creating models that represent the structure of sentences. Semantics deals with the meaning of a sentence that is determined by the meanings of its constituent parts and their syntactic relations. Thus, *John is playing golf* differs in meaning from *John is playing tennis*, regardless of the message either conveys in a particular context. The basic meaning of the sentence is determined by the combination of the constituent parts. This is the semantic interpretation of the sentence. Semantics, however, does not provide enough information to specify in a particular context the meaning of an utterance that consists of the same sequence of words. In fact, syntacticians and semanticists (in the narrow sense) are not interested in the context.

Utterances are produced at a specific time and place by a particular speaker. Many utterances do not conform to the grammatical rules that syntacticians specify. So an utterance may consist of a single noun (*John!*) or a verb without any indication of tense (*Coming!*) or an adverbial expression (*Down the hatch!*), though most utterances will contain some of the structures that syntacticians examine. Whatever the form, Pragmatics is concerned with what the speaker is doing in producing an utterance and how the listener can interpret the message. It will be obvious that much of what has been examined in this chapter belongs in pragmatics rather than semantics, and this also reflects the shift from a **formalist** approach to a **functional** one in syntax (see Chapter 3). Pragmatics, however, retains the goal of identifying the general principles of utterances rather than dealing with actual situations. The latter will be examined in Chapters 4 and 5.

## The meaning of meaning

Many heavy (in both senses) books have been written about semantics and pragmatics. The material covered in this chapter merely skims the surface of the subject, but it may give an idea of the difficulty of defining the notion "meaning." Like everything else connected to human language, it is extremely complex and yet for the most part we appear to communicate with each other very smoothly and without any strain. Whatever language is and however it is stored in the brain, it is a highly effective system for communication between human beings. The physiological process of speech that makes this possible will be examined in the next chapter.

## SUGGESTIONS FOR FURTHER READING

Published posthumously from notes made of his lectures, Ferdinand de Saussure's *Cours de Linguistique Générale* is still fascinating in its exploration of the problems of describing language. There are translations into English by Wade Baskins and by Roy Harris. A good account of semantics can be found in John Lyons *Linguistic Semantics* and important aspects of pragmatics are presented in Stephen Levinson's *Pragmatics* and *Presumptive Meanings*, but neither is easy reading for those unaccustomed to the field. A less challenging but also less comprehensive work is Frank Palmer's *Semantics*. John Austin's *How to do things with words* gave the impetus for much of the study of pragmatics and is very easy to read.

The problems of drawing a line between semantics and pragmatics are examined in a number of scholarly articles in Claudia Biachi *The Semantics/Pragmatics Distinction*. William Croft and Alan Cruse *Cognitive Linguistics* includes a good discussion of polysemy as well as metaphor, but it is written for fellow linguists rather than the general public. George Lakoff and Mark Johnson deal with the latter in *Metaphors we live by*, a book that does not require any knowledge of linguistics. The use of metaphor in poetry is examined by George Lakoff and Mark Turner in *More than cool reason*, which also does not use linguistic technical language. Sarcasm and other topics are dealt with in a very readable style by John Haiman in *Talk is Cheap*.

Dan Sperber and Deirdre Wilson's *Relevance: Communication and Cognition* gives a clear account of Relevance Theory. Robyn Carson's *Thoughts and Utterances* provides further elaboration of this view, including the understanding of metaphors. Ira Noveck and Dan Sperber's *Experimental Pragmatics* contains accounts of various psychological experiments on pragmatic questions.

# 2

# Language as Sound

```
. in the beginning was the word .
in thi beginning was thi wurd
in thi beginnin was thi wurd
in thi biginnin was thi wurd
in thi biginnin wuz thi wurd
n thi biginnin wuz thi wurd
nthi biginnin wuzthi wurd
nthibiginnin wuzthiwurd
nthibiginninwuzthiwurd
. in the beginning was the sound .
```

Tom Leonard

## Spoken language

In the previous chapter, Ferdinand de Saussure's diagram was used to illustrate his notion of meaning. His diagram of communication is reproduced in Figure 2.1.

The figure shows an arrow from A tracing a path from A's brain to his mouth and then to B's ear and then to his brain (the hairstyles suggest male figures). Saussure explains that the process begins with a concept in A's brain that is linked with a word. The word consists of a meaning and what Saussure calls a "sound-image," namely how that word is pronounced. This is a psychological process. The next stage is to send instructions to the parts of the body involved in producing speech. This, according to Saussure, is a physiological process. This process produces a disturbance of

the airwaves that is perceived by B, who employs a complementary physiological process to transmit the signal from the outer ear
to his brain, where the "sound-image" is interpreted as a concept
that, if all has gone well, should correspond to the concept that A
began with.

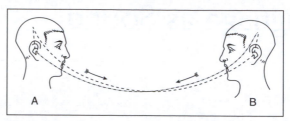

Figure 2.1    Saussure's diagram of communication

The diagram provides a very simple representation of what is
in fact a remarkable ability that human beings have developed for
communicating quickly, accurately, and for the most part without
conscious effort. Communication by means of speech would be
much more problematic if it were not for the fact that so much
of the process is automatic. But this skill comprises a complex
coordination of about a hundred muscles to produce speech and
a complex auditory process to understand it. The purpose of this
chapter is to outline some of the physiological and acoustic factors
that are involved in speech communication. As Saussure's diagram
indicates, there are three aspects of the situation, each of which
can be studied separately. One is the articulatory process by which
speech sounds are produced. Another is the acoustic signal itself.
The third is speech perception, the process by which the sounds are
interpreted as language. It is sometimes difficult to deal with one
of these aspects of the situation without referring to another.

Saussure also points out that neither thought nor the acoustic
signal has natural divisions that correspond to linguistic units. He
uses an analogy from the natural world showing the relationship
between the wind and wave formation and provides Figure 2.2.

There are parallel movements between the wind and the waves
similar to the correspondence between thought and speech. In
what Saussure calls a mysterious way, somehow a correspondence between sound and thought is achieved to create linguistic
units. Thus, the paradox about speech is that it is produced in a

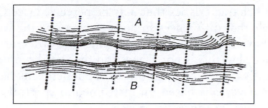

Figure 2.2    Saussure's wind and wave diagram

continuous stream but is interpreted segmentally. The question
*Did you say pig or fig?* assumes that there is a significant difference between the form *pig* and the form *fig.* Since the *–ig* part
is taken to be the same, the signaling difference must lie in the
difference between *p* and *f.* It is on the basis of reasoning like
this that linguists establish the set of signaling features that distinguish possible words. The sounds of a language that are capable of distinguishing words in this way are known as **phonemes**
(though there are disagreements about how the term should be
interpreted). However, in the stream of speech, sounds are not as
distinct as they appear in writing. It is easy to be misled by written symbols into taking an oversimplified view of the nature of
speech (see Chapter 7). It is one of the aims of the present chapter
to bring out some of the complexity of the physical process of
speech communication.

## The articulation of sounds

It is axiomatic in linguistics that there are no genetic characteristics that affect the ability to articulate sounds. The language
that you speak and how you speak it will depend upon the language that you are exposed to at the critical time in infancy and
childhood. The language of your genetic parents will not affect
this development, if you happen to be brought up in a different
environment from theirs. On the other hand, since speech is a
physiological process, body size and type will affect the actual
production of speech sounds. The most obvious example is the
age of the speaker. It is usually easy to tell when a speaker is quite
young or very old from the acoustic signal alone. It is also often
(but not always) easy to distinguish male speakers from female
speakers, often because of the pitch of the voice, and there are

other social characteristics that may be perceived (see Chapter 5). It is possible that differences in body size among the world's peoples may have had an influence on the way different languages have evolved, but this is not a question that has been investigated systematically. Much of the work that phoneticians have carried out in recent years is based on instrumental spectral analysis of the sound waves produced in speech.

Spectrographic analysis is often used to identify variation in vowels. Two concentrations of energy in the articulation of vowels appear as dark bands on a spectrogram. The lower band is known as the first formant and the next highest as the second formant, and these are the features most commonly investigated in looking at social variation in vowels. The example below is from my own speech. As someone who grew up in Scotland, I pronounce the diphthong /ay/ in *tied*, slightly longer than in *tide*, and much longer than in *tight*. You can see (in Figure 2.3) in (a) *tied* the first formant (the lower dark band) remaining steady to begin with and then rising near the end. In (b) *tide* the first formant starts to rise before halfway, and in (c) *tight* the first formant starts to rise immediately.

This kind of **acoustic analysis** is very useful for identifying small differences in sounds, as in my pronunciation of the diphthongs but it is too complicated to present adequately in a chapter of this kind, so I will concentrate on the physiological aspects of the production and comprehension of sounds, rather than on the actual acoustic signal.

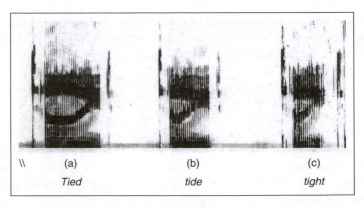

| \\        | (a)       | (b)       | (c)       |
|           | *Tied*    | *tide*    | *tight*   |

Figure 2.3    Spectrogram of tied, tide, tight

## The articulation process

Speech is modified breathing. Most speech sounds (though not all) are produced with the force of air expelled from the lungs. This is not something that we normally pay much attention to, unless we are engaging in energetic physical effort at the same time, and find ourselves short of breath, but fluent speech depends upon the regular flow of air from the lungs. Speaking, however, requires more physical effort than simply breathing and the chest muscles are actively involved in expelling air from the lungs. Limitations on the amount of air that can be comfortably exhaled in relaxed circumstances help to explain why people usually speak in "breath groups" of five to six words at the most. This physical limitation on speech production also helps in speech perception since the listener has to deal with stretches of sound that can easily be accommodated in short-term memory.

The airstream produced by the lungs is modified by various "moving parts" that are controlled by different muscles (Figure 2.4). There are the **vocal cords**, located in the larynx, protected by the thyroid cartilage that is known as Adam's apple. The space between the vocal cords is known as the **glottis**. Other movable parts are the tongue, the lips, and a small flap at the back of the throat known as the **velum**. The enormous variety of sounds produced in the world's six thousand

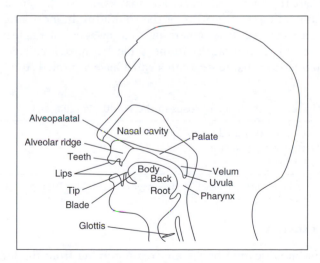

Figure 2.4  Diagram of the vocal tract

or more languages are the result of combining tiny movements of the muscles that control these moving parts. A few of these movements, such as opening and closing the lips, or putting the tongue against the roof of the mouth, are easy to control consciously, but most of the movements occur without direct conscious control.

## Aspirated consonants

For example, when an English speaker says the word *pin* the lips are initially closed to make the sound [p] and then opened to allow the pronunciation of the vowel. The same sequence occurs in uttering the word *spin*. However, there is an important difference that most English speakers are not aware of, unless they have taken a course in linguistics. In the case of *pin*, there is a brief interval after the lips are opened before the vowel is sounded. If you listen carefully you can hear a slight puff of air before the vowel. Phoneticians call this "aspiration" and the [p] an **aspirated consonant**. This puff of air does not occur after the [p] in *spin* and phoneticians say that this [p] is **unaspirated**. English speakers have learned to make this difference automatically and consistently without noticing it. (You can test this by holding a lighted match close to your mouth and saying the word *spin*; the flame will hardly move. Then say the word *pin*; in this case the flame will flicker and may even go out.) This aspiration is not an essential feature of the sound [p]. In most languages [p] is not aspirated. It is something that speakers of English have learned to do. As you can see in the Table 2.1, most languages have unaspirated stops but fewer than a third have aspirated stops.

Table 2.1  Frequency of stops in the world's languages

| | |
|---|---|
| Voiceless unaspirated stops | 92% |
| Voiceless aspirated stops | 29% |
| Voiced stops | 67% |

*Source*: Based on a sample of 317 languages at the UCLA Phonetics Lab

## Voiced sounds

The first modification of the airstream coming from the lungs in the production of vowels is the vibration of the vocal cords. The vocal cords are like a pair of lips in that they can be completely open, completely closed, or loosely closed. When they are completely open, the airstream can pass freely through; when tightly closed, the airstream cannot pass through. When the vocal cords are loosely closed and the airstream is forced through, they produce a buzzing sound in a similar fashion to a "raspberry" produced by the lips (though the effect is somewhat different). It is this buzzing sound that produces what phoneticians call **voice**. (You can hear this buzzing if you cover your ears with your hands and utter the sound [zzzzzzzz], but you will not hear it if you make the sound [ssssssss].) All sounds that are produced with the vocal cords vibrating are called **voiced** sounds and those when the vocal cords are not vibrating are said to be **voiceless**.

### Aspiration revisited

To return to the difference between *pin* and *spin*, what happens in the case of the [p] in *pin* is that the vocal cords do not start vibrating for the vowel until a brief period after the lips open, because the vocal cords are too far apart to vibrate. In the case of *spin* the vocal cords have come together and start vibrating at the same time as the lips open. This is not something that English speakers do consciously. In fact, most speakers find it difficult to reverse the process and delay the vibrating of the vocal cords after the [p] in *spin*. It is, of course, easy for them to start the vocal cords vibrating at the time the lips open, because that is what they do in uttering the word *bin*.

The difference between *pin* and *bin* illustrates another interesting aspect of speech production. The English writing system indicates that there is a difference between the initial sound [p] and the initial sound [b] in these words. However, there is practically no difference between the two sounds acoustically. What distinguishes these two words is not the difference between [p] and [b] but the presence or absence of the puff of air (aspiration) before the following vowel.

### Voice Onset Time

Another way of describing this is in terms of **Voice Onset Time** (VOT). VOT is the interval between the opening of the lips (in the case of [p] and [b]) and the beginning of the vibration of the vocal cords for the following vowel. There is little or no interval in the case of [b] in *bit*, but there is a perceptible interval in the case of [p] in *pit*. The interval is very short, on average about 50–70 milliseconds (0.05–0.07 of a second) in English, but it affects the perception of the consonant, and even infants at the age of a few months can detect the difference.

## Voiceless stops

As mentioned earlier, the airstream coming from the lungs is modified in various ways and these modifications result in what the listener perceives to be different sounds, but the differences are not necessarily those that the writing system might suggest. The consonants [p], [t], and [k] are an interesting example of this. All three are voiceless consonants, that is, the vocal cords are not vibrating during their articulation. All three are what is known as **stop consonants**, that is, the airstream is totally interrupted by a closure in the vocal tract. In the case of [p] the closure is made by the lips (bilabial); in the case of [t] (alveolar) and [k] (velar) by parts of the tongue against different positions in the roof of the mouth. During the closure no sound is produced. Thus the acoustic result is silence, and there is no difference between [p] and [t], for example, during the period of closure. Yet, we clearly hear a difference. The difference lies in the part that we can hear, namely the following (or preceding) vowel.

As will be described below, vowels differ according to the shape of the tongue in the mouth. What happens in the articulation of the word *pin* is that the tongue is free to assume the position for the following vowel, since the closure for the consonant is made with the lips. In the case of the word *tin*, the tongue takes the position for the consonant [t] and then has to move to the position for the following vowel. In the case of the word *kin*, the tongue makes contact further back in the mouth before moving to the position for the following vowel. Thus, what guides the listener's ear is not the difference between the sounds of [p], [t], and [k] (since there is essentially no difference) but the difference between the vowel following [p], the vowel following [t], and the vowel following [k]. As in the case of the difference between the initial consonants of *pin* and *bin*, we hear a difference but the difference is actually not signaled by differences in the sounds represented by the letters, as we might expect, but by modifications of the following vowel in the articulation of the words. Similar modifications affect the vowel when it occurs before consonants such as [p], [t], and [k]. Another way of looking at this comes from acoustic analysis. In a syllable such as *key*, there is no way to say when the sound of the consonant ends and the sound of the vowel begins. In contrast, it is much easier to say when the syllable begins and ends. We have learned from the alphabetic system of writing (see Chapter 7) to separate consonants from vowels, but that does not mean that we produce or recognize them separately.

## Voiced stops

In English the consonants [p], [t], and [k] are known as voiceless consonants, and the consonants [b], [d], and [g] as voiced consonants, but in fact in English the vocal cords usually do not vibrate during the articulation of [b], [d], and [g]. As was pointed out above, initial [p] is distinguished from initial [b] by aspiration (VOT). In medial and final position the difference is signaled by the timing of the vowel and the consonant. In words such as *lap* and *rapid* the preceding vowel is shorter and the closure for the consonant is longer compared to *lab* and *rabid* in which the vowel is longer and the closure for the consonant shorter. Once again, what we hear and what we see in the written form do not correspond exactly. Another way of putting this is that we treat certain sounds as if they were *different* when they are very *similar*, and we treat other sounds as *similar* when they are actually *distinct*. This is a fundamental problem in analyzing language at any level, form, meaning, and sound: when to identify two examples as "the same" or "different," in syntax (Chapter 3) and semantics (Chapter 1) as well as in phonetics.

The lack of voicing in the so-called voiced stops in English is not the case in all languages; for example, in French the vocal cords do vibrate during the articulation of [b], [d], and [g]. Other languages (e.g., Thai, Korean) have different voicing distinctions in stop consonants from those that we find in English.

## Other stop consonants

Some African languages have consonants during which the glottis is lowered before the release of the consonant, giving what sounds like a very strong voicing sound. Such consonants are known as **implosives**. Other languages have stop consonants in which the glottis is raised before the release, producing an extra force in the articulation of voiceless consonants. These sounds are known as **ejectives**. Even further from English consonants are the **click sounds** found in a small number of African languages. These are produced by making two closures between the tongue and the roof of the mouth and using the air trapped there to produce consonants. When the more forward closure is released a sharp noise is produced. This is how English speakers produce the nonverbal sign of disapproval *tsk tsk*, but in Zulu and Xhosa such sounds are used as consonants to distinguish words, just as [p], [t], and [k] are in English. There can be as many as eighty different kinds of clicks used in African languages.

Table 2.2   Frequency of ejectives and implosives in the world's languages

| | |
|---|---|
| Ejectives | 16% |
| Implosives | 11% |

*Source*: Based on a sample of 317 languages at the UCLA Phonetics Lab

Stop consonants are comparatively easy to describe, for a variety of reasons. One is proprioceptive feedback. If someone asks you how you produce the initial sound in *tin*, you can start to say the word and feel where the tip of your tongue touches the roof of your mouth, somewhere just behind the teeth. It may be a little more difficult to say where the back of the tongue touches during the production of the consonant [k], partly because the back of the tongue provides a less clear indication of where the contact is made. In fact, you may not find it easy to distinguish where the tongue makes contact with the roof of the mouth in saying *keep*, compared with where the contact occurs in saying *cool*. In the case of *cool* the contact is further back in the mouth than it is for *keep*, because of the influence of the following vowel.

## Palatography

There is also a useful technique called **palatography** that has been used to identify where the contact is made between the tongue and the roof of the mouth. In one version of this procedure, the tongue is coated with a black paste that adheres to the roof of the mouth when the sound is articulated. By looking at the residue on the roof of the mouth, the investigator can tell where the contact was made; by looking at where the paste has been wiped off, it is possible to see which part of the tongue made contact. This technique has been employed in identifying the characteristics of stop consonants in a wide range of languages.

Techniques such as palatography and other instrumental methods have been very useful in collecting information on the variety of consonants found in the languages of the world. In English there are three positions in which stop consonants are produced: **labial** [p] and [b] (with the lips), **alveolar** [t] and [d] (tip of the tongue against the alveolar ridge, just behind the teeth), and **velar** [k] and [g] (back of the tongue against the roof of the mouth, near the velum). In some varieties of English there is a fourth location and that is in the glottis where sudden closure and release of the vocal cords will produce a **glottal stop**. (This is the sound that many speakers of American English use instead of [t] in words such as *mountain*.) In many languages, however, there are more than three or four positions in which stop consonants can be produced, including sounds produced by contact between the root of the tongue and the back wall of the pharynx. There are sixteen different places in the vocal tract where consonants can be produced, including (rarely) epiglottal stops. Table 2.3 shows that almost all the languages of the world have bilabial, dental/alveolar, and velar stop consonants, while stops made elsewhere are rarer.

Table 2.3   Frequency of types of consonants in the world's languages

| Bilabial | 99.1% |
| --- | --- |
| Dental or alveolar | 99.7% |
| Palatal | 18.6% |
| Velar | 99.4% |
| Uvular | 14.8% |

*Source*: Based on a sample of 317 languages at the UCLA Phonetics Lab

Phoneticians have been studying the variety of stop consonants in the world's languages for many years but they are still not sure that they have successfully identified all the possibilities. The variety and subtlety of many distinctions underlines the incredible flexibility of the human body in developing different ways in which to communicate orally.

## Other consonants

In addition to stop consonants, there are other consonants such as **fricatives, affricates, laterals, trills,** and **nasals.** Discussing all of them would go beyond the scope and purpose of the present chapter, which is mainly to give an indication of the vast complexity of the human vocal apparatus, but a brief description of one type of fricative will illustrate another aspect of the system. Stop consonants are both easier to produce and to describe since they involve contact between two articulators, and slight differences in where the contact is made are unlikely to affect communication in most cases. The articulation of many fricatives requires greater articulatory precision. Fricative sounds are produced when the airstream is forced through a narrow passage causing turbulence that is perceived as a continuous noise. The final sound in *hiss* is an example of a fricative in English. The production of the [s] sound requires the tongue to be moved to a certain distance from the roof of the mouth and held there steadily during the articulation of the sound.

The greater degree of control necessary to utter a fricative sound such as [s] in contrast to a stop consonant such as [t] can be illustrated by a simple physical task. Put your first finger and thumb together. This action is very easy to carry out and requires little conscious attention, and you can keep them there with no effort. Now, put your thumb and finger together at a distance no greater than the width of a sheet of paper. This action requires concentration and effort to maintain the small distance without making contact between the two. This is the kind of muscular control necessary to produce a sound such as [s]. If you allow the tongue to get so close to the roof of the mouth that it makes contact, you will have a stop consonant instead of a fricative. If you allow the tongue to move too far away from the roof of the mouth, there will no longer be a narrow enough passage to produce the turbulence and the hissing sound. Moreover, if you raise the back of your tongue slightly you will produce not the final sound in *hiss* but the final sound in *hush*. Yet we are able to produce these sounds without any sense of the effort we put into holding our finger and thumb close together without touching. We have developed the neurological control to the point where it is unconscious and automatic. It is not surprising that it takes young children longer to master all the fricatives than it does to control the stop consonants.

The range of consonants in the languages of the world can be seen in the chart produced by the International Phonetic Association (Figure 2.5).

**CONSONANTS (PULMONIC)** © 2005 IPA

| | Bilabial | Labiodental | Dental | Alveolar | Postalveolar | Retroflex | Palatal | Velar | Uvular | Pharyngeal | Glottal |
|---|---|---|---|---|---|---|---|---|---|---|---|
| Plosive | p b | | | t d | | ʈ ɖ | c ɟ | k g | q ɢ | | ʔ |
| Nasal | m | ɱ | | n | | ɳ | ɲ | ŋ | ɴ | | |
| Trill | ʙ | | | r | | | | | ʀ | | |
| Tap or Flap | | ⱱ | | ɾ | | ɽ | | | | | |
| Fricative | ɸ β | f v | θ ð | s z | ʃ ʒ | ʂ ʐ | ç ʝ | x ɣ | χ ʁ | ħ ʕ | h ɦ |
| Lateral fricative | | | | ɬ ɮ | | | | | | | |
| Approximant | | ʋ | | ɹ | | ɻ | j | ɰ | | | |
| Lateral approximant | | | | l | | ɭ | ʎ | ʟ | | | |

Figure 2.5    IPA consonant chart

*Note*: Where symbols appear in pairs, the one to the right represents a voiced consonant. Shaded areas denote articulations judged impossible.

*Source*: Reproduced by permission of the International Phonetic Association

## Vowels

The degree of fine motor control needed to produce fricatives is remarkable but an even finer control is needed to make the distinctions that are necessary to produce a range of vowels. Vowels are produced with the vocal cords vibrating and no obstruction in the vocal tract. (In some languages voiceless vowels occur but only in restricted environments; there is no language with only voiceless vowels.) The differences in vowel sounds mainly come from a combination of three factors. The first is the height of the tongue in the mouth: high, mid, or low. The second factor is which part of the tongue is highest: front, central, or back. The third factor is whether the lips are spread or rounded. In general, front vowels are produced with the lips spread and are known as **unrounded vowels**; back vowels are usually produced with the lips rounded and are known as **rounded vowels**. (There are also rounded front vowels and unrounded back vowels, but they are much less common, found in a limited number of languages, and each accounting for only about 5% of the vowels in the languages of the world.) The vowel in *feed* is a high front unrounded vowel; the vowel in *food* is a high back rounded vowel. Figure 2.6 is the chart from The International Phonetic Alphabet for the description of the sounds of any language.

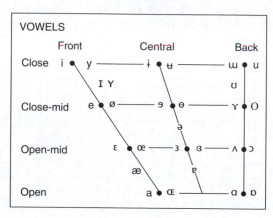

Figure 2.6    IPA vowel diagram

*Note*: Where symbols appear in pairs, the one to the right represents a rounded vowel.

*Source*: Reproduced with permission of the International Phonetic Association.

In contrast to most consonants, vowels are more difficult to identify in articulatory terms. The sound [p] is universally produced by closing the lips, and there is little scope for variation between languages, so that the sound [p] in one language can be equated with the sound [p] in an unrelated language. The situation is very different with vowels. Languages vary in the number of vowels they distinguish, ranging from three to twenty-four. The majority of languages have at least three vowel sounds with two high vowels /i/ and /u/ and one low vowel /a/ (Table 2.4).

Table 2.4    Frequency of most common vowels in the world's languages

| | |
|---|---|
| /i/ | 92% |
| /a/ | 88% |
| /u/ | 84% |

*Source*: Based on a sample of 317 languages at the UCLA Phonetics Lab

The fewer vowels that a language has the greater the range of variation that is possible for each of them. One way of looking at the situation is to consider the space in the mouth in which the tongue can move as if it were a plot of land. If there are only five vowels in a language, the space is divided up into five regions, if seven vowels, then seven regions, but they will be smaller. Each vowel is free to vary within its territory. All that is necessary to keep the vowels distinct is that one vowel should not encroach too far on another's territory, but in fact there is usually some overlap with neighboring vowels. Vowels are not as clearly separate from each other as most consonants are. This also means that it is difficult to make cross-linguistic comparisons between them. A high front unrounded vowel in one language (e.g., Spanish) may occupy the same vocalic space as two vowels in another language (e.g., English). This makes any claims about the universal characteristics of vowels somewhat problematic.

Another way of putting it is that there are no firm boundaries between vowels. For example, many speakers of American English pronounce the names *Dawn* and *Don* as markedly different while other speakers pronounce them as exactly the same. Such differences are an example of dialect differences, but there is also a change taking place (see Chapter 5). Some people who used to keep these words (and others with the same vowels) distinct now pronounce them the same, but when asked whether they say them the same or different, some people will claim to make a distinction that their hearers cannot perceive. There is a paradox here. Speakers make very fine distinctions in the vowels that they utter and they are also capable of detecting fine distinctions in the speech of others, but they are often unaware of the precise character of the vowel sounds that they use. Another example comes from a study in Philadelphia where some speakers who make a distinction between the words *ferry* and *furry* in their speech cannot hear the difference when the examples are played back to them. This lack of awareness helps to explain why until recently many people were often surprised (and sometimes shocked) when they heard themselves on tape.

## Speech perception

The example of English voiceless consonants given earlier illustrates a more general point about speech perception. We identify

differences as belonging to certain parts of the acoustic signal
when in fact the differences are carried by a different part of the
signal. We treat some sounds as different when in fact they are
the same and treat others as different when they are very similar
to each other, if not identical. It is not, however, surprising that
this should be the case. Peter Ladefoged carried out an experiment with synthesized speech. He synthesized a monosyllabic
word beginning with [b] and ending in [t] and a vowel between
them. He then played this synthesized word to a number of subjects in the context of a synthesized instruction *Please say what
this word is.* Both the word and the instruction were judged to
sound more or less like a normal human voice speaking. Because
this was synthesized speech, it was possible to modify the instruction sentence systematically so that it sounded as if it had been
recorded by different speakers. As a result of these modifications,
the listeners identified the test word sometimes as *bit* or *bet,* sometimes as *bat* or *but.* In other words, what was in fact the same
sound was perceived as different words depending upon the form
in which the instruction was given. The listeners were adjusting
their ears to fit their expectations of how the speaker who gave
the instruction would say the test word. Moreover, the listeners
spoke different regional dialects (see Chapter 5) and differed in
their own form of speech and these differences affected how they
perceived the test word. Although these results were obtained
with synthesized speech, a later experiment with natural voices
confirmed the finding.

Another experiment was carried out with speakers who were
bilingual in Swedish and English. The experimenter played the listeners recordings that included a series of words, such as *sit, set,
sat,* and *sot.* When the bilinguals were asked in English to report
what they heard, they could distinguish all four forms. When they
were asked in Swedish, they could not distinguish *set* from *sat,*
because that is not a contrast in the form of Swedish they spoke.
As in the other experiment, the listeners were influenced by their
expectations of the speaker's language.

These were experimental demonstrations of an ability that all
human beings have, which is to calibrate the acoustic signal that
they hear with the pitch of the speaker's voice. We hear a variety of
voices from children to elderly people, of both sexes, and of varied
body size. The pitch of the voice is to some extent affected by the

length of the vibrating part of the vocal cords (longer in males) and there are other factors that are influenced by the size of the vocal tract. This means that the "same" word spoken by different people need not be the same acoustically. Yet, we seldom have difficulty in identifying the words that people in our community say. Where we are more likely to have difficulty is with speakers of a different dialect (Chapter 5). That is because we have not trained our ears to process their speech as automatically as we do that of our friends and neighbors.

## The stream of speech

Linguists have tended to pay most attention to those aspects of speech that can be easily transcribed into an alphabetic notation, and this gives a misleading impression of the physiological process of speech production. The conventional form for writing English may give the impression that the sounds in some words are more distinct than they are in normal speech. For example, in the word *handsome* the [d] is never pronounced, a non-native speaker who pronounced the [d] would sound slightly odd. In the word *hand-kerchief* the [d] is not pronounced either but here the loss of the [d] results in the first syllable being pronounced like *hang*. This change is the result of the influence of the following [k] on the preceding [n], a process known as **assimilation**. Every introductory linguistics textbook includes a variety of examples to illustrate this process, but focusing on the process as a result of combining sounds may give a misleading impression of the speech process.

Formal linguists (Chapter 3) present the structure of language as a set of discrete elements that can be combined into units of various kinds, for example, words can be combined into phrases. Linguists who take a formal approach to the sounds of speech (phonologists) tend to take a similar approach of combining discrete sounds (phonemes) into combinations (words), and there are numerous phonological theories about this process. There is, however, a basic problem in that there is no evidence that speakers begin with discrete sounds in the physiological process of producing an utterance. There is also no reason to believe that listeners process what they hear in terms of the individual sounds that make up the words. Spoken utterances are produced as a continuous stream of sound not as a succession of discrete consonants and vowels. It is only where there is a problem in trying to comprehend what has been said that listeners may need to identify individual sounds. In most normal conversation (Chapter 4), however, communication takes place without either speaker or hearer paying close attention to the individual sounds that make up the utterance. On the other hand, listeners are very quick to pick up the small differences in the signals that reflect our membership in various social categories (Chapter 5).

Just as syntacticians have perhaps paid too much attention to rules for combining words into syntactic structures (Chapter 3), so have phoneticians probably devoted too much effort into examining how sounds are combined into words. Both attitudes have presumably been induced by the powerful influence of an alphabetic writing system. The development of an alphabetic system for writing down speech (see Chapter 7) has been such an important factor in the development of Western civilization that it would be hard to exaggerate its significance. Yet its very success seems to have misled many people into confusing the representation of language in written form with how it is stored in the brain for the production of speech.

All normal human beings learn to speak and understand spoken language long before they learn to read and write it (if they ever do). An overwhelming majority of the people who have lived on this earth did not learn how to read or write. They could not have done so, since writing is a relatively recent invention in the history of mankind, and even in literate societies (at least until recently) most people were illiterate. Obviously, the various forms of language that these people spoke must have been stored in the brain in a form that did not depend upon such features as alphabetic symbols. Moreover, the language must be stored in a form that allows rapid, automatized processing in real time. As literate adults, we tend to think of language in written terms. When we are trying to find a word or recall a name, we may say things like "It begins with a B" and mentally run through a list like the entries in a dictionary. We must have some mental storage of how words are spelled because we recognize them quickly in print and know how to write them correctly. There is also evidence from speech errors that literate speakers have a representation of words that includes the order of sounds, but opinions differ as to the significance of such a phenomenon. We have, in fact, no privileged introspective knowledge of how the language that we use when we speak is stored in our brains.

## Prosodic features

Another indication that linguists have been influenced by the alphabetical system is the relative neglect of the study of **prosodic features**. Prosody includes the rise and fall of the **pitch** of the utterance (**intonation**), **rhythm** and **stress**, none of which is indicated in the writing system (except for such devices as the use of italics for special emphasis). These are all essential features of speech and they can affect the meaning of the message just as significantly as the words and structures used.

Stress is the term used with reference to the degree of prominence of a syllable in a polysyllabic word. This can be seen in the following related words in which the stressed syllable is indicated by capital letters: *PHOTograph, phoTOGraphy, photoGRAPHic.* Stress is also used in English to distinguish verbs from nouns, as in *to inSULT,* in contrast to *an INsult.*

Intonation functions differently in different languages. In English a rising intonation at the end of an utterance may convert a possible statement into a question. *John is really smart?* is more likely to suggest doubts than confidence in John's ability.

An obvious example is the use of sarcasm or irony (see Chapter 1), where an utterance such as *That was clever* may convey exactly the contrary of the meaning of the words. Intonation serves among other functions to indicate how confident the speaker is. Many disputes have arisen because of an assumption that *No* did not really mean "no." Intonation may also give an indication of the speaker's attitude. Sometimes, congratulations, praise, or sympathy may seem hollow because of the tone of voice in which they are expressed.

Prosodic features also accompany expressions of anger, joy, fear, and other emotions. Linguists have tended to leave the study of such matters to social psychologists or conversation analysts (see Chapter 4), but affect is an essential part of speech and therefore ought to be of concern to those who are trying to understand language. Speed of articulation is another feature that seldom receives attention from linguists, but the acoustic signal in rapid speech is very different from that of slow, deliberate utterances. If we wish to understand how the human brain processes speech, we need to know what the limits are in terms of speed of articulation. Many people have had the experience of listening to a very slow, hesitant speaker and know how much more difficult it is to follow what is being said than if the speech rate were normal. Similarly, very fast talkers can sometimes cause problems of a different kind. Differences in speech rate and intonation can contribute to misunderstanding between members of different speech communities (see Chapter 5). Rhythmic factors can also play an important role in conversation (Chapter 4).

Linguists naturally focus their attention on the linguistic aspects of speech perception and this gives an oversimplified view of the communication event. It is true that we pay attention to what someone is saying in order to understand the message, but at the same time we are processing other information. We can often tell the mood of a speaker from the quality of the acoustic signal quite independently of the linguistic message. When a speaker is tense, or anxious, or exhausted, there are likely to be signs in the quality of their speech. Such emotions as anger and joy are often signaled by tone of voice as much as by the content of the speech. We are all aware of this but the focus of linguists on the linguistic features of speech generally ignores these other aspects but we process both the linguistic message and its affect at the same time. We do not process the linguistic message and then pay attention to the affect with which it is communicated. We do both at the same time. Ignoring the emotional aspect of speech underestimates the remarkable ability of the human brain to process so much information simultaneously and effortlessly. It can also lead investigators into children's language development to misunderstand the challenge that children face. Children are not only developing knowledge of the language they are exposed to, they are also at the same time learning how to interpret the clues that speech gives about the attitude of the speakers.

One of Saussure's aims was to create a place for linguistics as a separate discipline, independent of psychology or sociology. Almost a hundred years later this goal has clearly been achieved but there are increasing signs that the independence of linguistics as a discipline may have come at heavy price. Saussure, Chomsky, and formal linguists deal with an idealized form of language, kept distinct from the complex aspects of how language is used in real life communication situations. Even phoneticians, who have employed a range of empirical methods in their investigation of speech, have tended to deal with individual words or short phrases, often recorded in the unnatural setting of a phonetics laboratory. Both the formal linguists and the phoneticians have been able to amass a great deal of information that contributes to our knowledge of language, but an increasing number of scholars have come to the conclusion that it is necessary to examine language use in more natural conditions in order to understand how the brain actually processes language.

Studies of language variation (see Chapter 5) and language communication (see Chapter 4) have shown that it is possible to study Saussure's **parole** ("use of language") empirically. It is no longer necessary to take the perspective of Chomsky's "ideal speaker-listener" (Chapter 3) or limit the notion of language to "the speech of one individual pronouncing in a definite and consistent style," as the pioneering phonetician Daniel Jones put it. New techniques of observation and experimentation make possible the study of speech as the dynamic process it is, rather than as a petrified fossil under a microscope. The number of scholars investigating the dynamic aspect of language has increased greatly in recent years, though the field is still dominated by those whose interest lies in abstract patterns. It is not yet clear how long that situation will continue.

## SUGGESTIONS FOR FURTHER READING

The easiest introduction is David Abercrombie's *Elements of General Phonetics*. Peter Ladefoged's *A Course in Phonetics* is designed as an introductory text and his *Phonetic Data Analysis* shows how phoneticians carry out their analysis. The most comprehensive account is Peter Ladefoged and Ian Maddieson's *The Sounds of the World's Languages*, though it is not designed for beginners. An even more technical account is given in Ian Maddison's *Patterns of Sound*. The statistics on frequency of consonants come from this work. Recent developments are discussed in a technical manner by Alain Marchal in *From Speech Pathology to Linguistics Phonetics* Alan Cruttenden's *Intonation* provides a useful account of the topic. *Intonation in Discourse* edited by Catherine Johns-Lewis examines the use of intonation in conversations. A.C.Gimson's pioneering *An Introduction to the Pronunciation of English* has been brought up-to-date by Alan Cruttenden in *Gimson's Pronunciation of English*. For American English the best account is Arthur Bronstein's *The Pronunciation of American English*. Tom Leonard's poem is from his collection *Intimate Voices*.

# 3

# Language as Form

Linguistics is the discipline that takes a scientific approach to the study of language. In 1924, Leonard Bloomfield published in the journal *Language* an article entitled "A set of postulates for the science of language." In this article he defined a language as "the totality of utterances that can be made in a speech community." He then defined an utterance as being made up "wholly of forms." By **form** he meant "a recurrent vocal feature which has meaning," of which the most obvious examples are words, though they are not the only kinds of meaningful forms. The notion of form is central to an understanding of the nature of human language.

In contrast, to animal communication, human language has the essential characteristic that parts of the message can be identified in terms of form. The question "Did you say *pig* or *fig*?" is a reasonable one because the words *pig* and *fig* are similar noises to some extent but differ in their initial sounds, as do some other words, such as *big, dig, rig,* and *wig,* and it is the difference in their initial sounds that makes it easy to distinguish them. Other words differ in their final sounds, for example, *pin, pit* and *fin, fit,* or differ in the vowel, for example, *pen, pan,* and *pun.* All human languages employ this formal device of distinguishing expressions and, as far as we know, it is absent from all kinds of animal communication. The study of the systematic use of speech sounds is **phonology,** but this chapter will not deal with that aspect of linguistic form.

Words such as *pig* and *fig* are forms that are complete in themselves and cannot be analyzed into smaller meaningful parts, but many other words contain separable units that carry a specific

47

meaning or function. For example, the word *pigs* consists of the word *pig* plus the suffix *-s* to indicate the notion of plural. The word *taller* consists of the adjective *tall* plus the suffix *-er* to indicate "more." It is not the case that all syllables express separate meanings. The word *hammer* does not include a suffix *-er* with a distinct meaning. The study of the ways in which words are constructed is **morphology**. Again, this is an important kind of linguistic form but it is a topic that will not be examined in this chapter.

## Syntax

Instead, the focus will be on **syntax**, the ways in which forms are combined to produce utterances. The study of syntax over the past fifty years has provided many very exciting (and controversial) insights into the structure of language. As will become apparent, this has not been a simple, gradual, cumulative progress. There have been dramatic leaps forward, followed by steps backward from earlier positions. Particularly in the years 1955–1970, the study of syntax was a lively and exciting field.

Any introductory linguistics class will make clear to the students that syntax is not simply a matter of combining words in a particular order. The units of syntax are abstract structures in which words are grouped into constituents. A simple example will illustrate the situation. Although the sentences (a) *he ran up a big bill* and (b) *he ran up a big hill* look very similar when considered as sequences of words, they have different syntactic structures. This can immediately be seen if the pronoun *it* is substituted for *a big bill* and *a big hill*. In (a) we would have *and he ran it up quickly* and in (b) *and he ran up it quickly*. In a similar kind of example *they decided on the boat* is ambiguous (at least in its written form) as to whether it means that they made their decision while on the boat or whether they chose the boat. These examples illustrate the notion of **constituent structure**. In the first example, *ran* + *up* are a constituent in (a), namely what is called a **phrasal verb**. In (b) the verb is *ran* and *up a hill* is a constituent, namely an **adverbial phrase**. In the second example, *on the boat* is a constituent (adverbial phrase) if that is where *they* made their decision, and *decided on* (phrasal verb) is a constituent where it refers to their choosing the boat. These are only simple examples to illustrate the notion of constituent structure. The study of syntax concerns the identification of a wide range of constituents and their relationships. This chapter explores some of the ways linguists have investigated syntactic structure in recent years.

## The Chomskyan revolution: Phase one

In 1957, an exciting new way of looking at language dramatically changed the field of linguistics with the publication of Noam Chomsky's *Syntactic Structures*. Prior to this time American linguists had shown only limited interest in syntax, concentrating their efforts more on phonology and morphology. Those linguists who dealt with syntax employed what is called **Immediate Constituent Analysis**, in which words were grouped according to their relationship, such as I indicated above for *up a hill* and *decided on*. These relationships can be shown in a diagram, known as a **Phrase Structure Tree**, as shown in Figure 3.1.

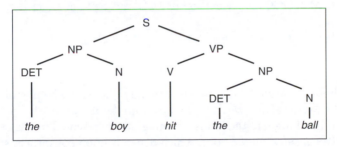

Figure 3.1   Phrase structure tree

   This diagram shows that *the boy* and *the ball* are **Noun Phrases** (**NP**), consisting of a **Noun** *boy* or *ball* and a **Determiner** *the*, while *hit the ball* is a **Verb Phrase** (**VP**), and the sentence (S) consists of a NP + VP. This diagram is a formal representation of the structure of the sentence *the boy hit the ball* but it is not a model of what speakers do, nor is it a direct representation of what speakers know. It is not necessary to know what a determiner (or even a noun or a verb) is in order to speak and understand English or any other language, but you have to know what items can combine with other items, in what ways, and with what effects. In other words, speakers must make use of constituent structure, whether they have any conscious knowledge of it or not. The example is a representation of a very simple syntactic structure. Speakers of any human language employ a wide range of syntactic structures, some of them very complex indeed. The challenge for linguists is to find a way of representing these structures in a coherent and consistent way that accounts for how speakers (of all languages) can employ them to express themselves.

---

You can test your awareness of constituent structure by substituting a pronoun or other general form for a sequence of words.

*The boy hit the ball* → *He did it quickly*

Here *he* is equivalent to *the boy* and *did it* to *hit the ball.*

What form could be substituted for the underlined phrases in the following examples?

a. *You can put it <u>in the corner</u>*

b. *He denied <u>that he had stolen the money</u>*

c. *John regrets <u>having told her</u>*

d. *Mary spoke angrily to Peter and John <u>spoke angrily to Peter too</u>*

[a = there; b =.it; c = it; d = did]

---

Chomsky tackled the problem of syntactic structure by postulating an abstract level that was not obvious from the actual words and their order. In addition to the kinds of ambiguity represented by the example *they decided on the boat*, which depends upon constituent structure, there are cases where a particular sequence of words can have different meanings. For example, Chomsky pointed out that a phrase such as *the shooting of the hunters* was ambiguous as to whether it referred to hunters doing the shooting or someone shooting the hunters. Chomsky proposed that there was an underlying structure for each of the meanings, one with the hunters as the **subject** of the verb *hunt* and one with the hunters as the **object** of the verb. He proposed an analysis in which all sentences were represented by an abstract underlying structure that might be very different from the superficial form of the sentence. This underlying structure was converted to its recognizable form by what he called **transformational rules**. This model came to be known as **Transformational Grammar**.

Chomsky also proposed that Phrase Structure trees for representing constituent structure, such as that in (1) could best be represented by a set of **Phrase Structure Rules** that applied sequentially: S → NP VP, VP → V NP, NP → DET N, and similarly for more complex structures. The rules were an algorithmic process that applied without appeal to meaning and the result of applying the rules **generated** the structure. "Generated" is simply a technical term for describing this process. It has nothing to do with the production of utterances. The model was often identified as a **Transformational-Generative Grammar** as shown in Figure 3.2.

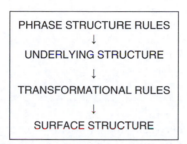

Figure 3.2    Diagram of Transformational-Generative Grammar

Chomsky employed transformations to relate sentences such as *the boy hit the ball* to its passive equivalent *the ball was hit by the boy*. He claimed that the two sentences had the same meaning and therefore should have the same underlying form. There were many other examples where different so-called **surface structures** could be related to the same underlying form, as in *it seems that John is unhappy* and *John seems to be unhappy*, or *Peter broke the vase* and *it was Peter who broke the vase* or *it was the vase that Peter broke* or *what Peter broke was the vase*. As with the relationship between **active** and **passive** sentences, the difference in word order in these sentences does not change the fundamental meaning (though there is a more subtle difference in emphasis).

It is difficult for younger linguists nowadays to understand just how exciting Chomsky's analysis was when it first appeared, because this had been a serious problem for earlier accounts of syntax. Chomsky's transformational approach could also be used to account for structural relationships in languages other than English.

Chomsky also suggested that many infinitival structures (i.e., those that have *to* before the verb) have an underlying sentence. For example, *John expects to pass the exam* comes from the same underlying structure as *John expects he will pass the exam*.

Since there are many infinitival constructions in English, this was an exciting idea, and it revealed several different kinds of infinitives.

---

**Some infinitival constructions in English**

John expects to pass the exam
John expects Mary to pass the exam
John believes Mary to be clever
John seems to be clever
John is eager to please
John is easy to please
It is easy to please John
Peter asked John what to buy
John told Peter to buy a pizza

---

The similarity between surface forms can conceal an underlying difference. For example, in the case of *John is eager to please*, John is eager to please someone else; in contrast, in *John is easy to please*, the person to be pleased is John. Chomsky demonstrated that such relationships could be shown economically through a system of what he called **kernel sentences** and transformations. Chomsky's analyses were very influential on many linguists at the time, though some of the older linguists remained skeptical.

---

**Some other examples of transformations**

*John helped Mary* → *Mary was helped by John*
*John sent a book to Mary* → *John sent Mary a book*
*That he knew the answer surprised us* → *It surprised us that he knew the answer*
*Mary bought a new dress at the market* → *It was Mary whot bought a new dress at the market*
*It was at the market that Mary bought a new dress* → *It was a new dress that Mary bought at the market*
*John told Peter all about it* → *What John did was tell Peter all about it*
*John did his homework in the morning* → *In the morning, John did his homework*
*All the boys stayed away from school* → *The boys all stayed away from school*

---

# The Chomskyan revolution:
# Phase two

As with any innovative approach, unforeseen problems soon emerged. One was that the transformations often changed the meaning, as when, for example, an affirmative kernel sentence was transformed into a question or a negative one. This required that the account of the sentence had to keep track of the transformations, which was an added complication. In his next major book *Aspects of the theory of Syntax* Chomsky accepted the notion that transformations should not change the meaning. Instead, all the meaningful elements were specified at the level of **Phrase Structure Rules**, which he now labeled **Deep Structure**, and this led to the inclusion of abstract features to represent such notions as **Negative** and **Interrogative**. These features did not represent words (or parts of words) in the same way as the examples in the earlier version.

In *Syntactic Structures*, Chomsky had claimed that "[g]rammar is best formulated as a self-contained study independent of semantics" (1957: 106), and had argued that sequences such as *colorless green ideas sleep furiously* were grammatical sentences in English. But in *Aspects of the Theory of Syntax*, he changed his view and introduced features that most people would consider semantic in order to subcategorize **lexical items** (i.e., words) and he used these features to limit the occurrence of categories of words in syntactic structures. For example, to deal with the acceptability of *sincerity may frighten the boy* compared with the unacceptable *\*the boy may frighten sincerity,* Chomsky also introduced semantic features such as Animate, Human, and Abstract, so that a word such as *boy* was [+Animate, +Human], while *dog* was [+Animate, –Human], and *sincerity* was [–Animate, +Abstract] and *dirt* was [–Animate, –Abstract]. The word *frighten* was marked as requiring a [+Animate] object, thus preventing sentences such as *\*the boy may frighten sincerity*. The asterisk \* is used to mark a sequence that is considered ungrammatical. This was a complete about-face from his earlier position, although its significance was not totally understood at the time.

| | |
|---|---|
| *Boy* | [+ Animate + Human] |
| *Dog* | [+Animate − Human] |
| *Book* | [−Animate − Abstract] |
| *Virtue* | [−Animate + Abstract] |
| *Dirt* | [−Animate − Abstract] |

In *Syntactic Structures* and writings before *Aspects of the Theory of Grammar*, Chomsky had presented a set of rules that were to be mechanically applied, that is, without appeal to the user's other knowledge. These rules were developed on the basis of a simple distinction between grammatical and ungrammatical sentences that any speaker of English could identify. He argued that on the basis of the "clear cases" it would be possible to establish the legitimacy of dubious examples. *Aspects* attempted to extend this model to a much more complex notion of language and the distinction between grammatical and ungrammatical became less obvious. Chomsky argued that "the speaker-listener's **linguistic intuition** is the ultimate standard that determines the accuracy of any proposed grammar." Unfortunately, for Chomsky (and linguistics in general) the speaker-listener's intuition turned out to be a less reliable guide to abstract structure than he had suggested, and the course of much subsequent work in Chomsky's framework was disrupted by disputes over linguistic intuitions and disagreements as to which examples were grammatical. Moreover, grammaticality judgments tend to reflect knowledge of the written language (see Chapter 7) and many utterances that would be acceptable in speech would not occur in writing.

It was in *Aspects of the Theory of Syntax* that Chomsky introduced the distinction between Deep Structure and Surface Structure. Roughly speaking, the Deep Structure provided all the information needed to understand the sentence and the Surface Structure provided the information on how it should be said (or written). The Deep Structure was interpreted by the **Semantic Component** to provide the meaning of the sentence, while the **Phonological Component** interpreted the Surface Structure to indicate how the sentence should be spoken (or written). In other words, the Deep Structure provided all the information needed to understand the sentence and the Surface Structure provided the information on how it should be said. (Chomsky's distinction was soon borrowed into a number of unrelated fields such as music and art history; later Chomsky employed the terms d-structure and s-structure to avoid the connotations of deep with profound and surface with superficial.) The Deep Structure level provided all the information necessary to make sure that the words would combine into a well-formed sentence such as *sincerity may frighten the boy* and exclude unacceptable sequences such as *\*the boy may frighten sincerity*.

The Deep Structure rules allowed the introduction of one sentence as a constituent of another, as in *Peter thinks (that) John escaped*, in which one sentence *John escaped* is **embedded** within another *John thinks*. These rules are recursive (i.e, they can apply more than once) so that more than one sentence can be embedded. The favorite example to illustrate this is the nursery rhyme: *This is the cat, that killed the rat, that ate the malt, that lay in the house that Jack built*, and so on. In its last verse there are twelve embedded sentences. This makes possible (in principle) much longer sentences than anyone would ever use, but the rules are one example of the ways in which human languages make use of a relatively small number of elements to produce a limitless number of expressions.

## The counter-revolution: Phase one
## Generative Semantics

At about this time in the mid-1960s there were other linguists investigating ways of representing syntactic structure who believed that Chomsky did not go far enough in incorporating semantic notions into syntactic analysis. These linguists (e.g., George Lakoff, Paul Postal, John Ross, and James McCawley) believed that it was a mistake to reify a syntactic level of Deep Structure different from the semantic representation of the sentence. They argued that all the meaning could be represented in a kind of logical form that was then transformed by a variety of rules into a surface structure, without the need for a separate level of Deep Structure. One of the principal differences was that the Generative Semanticists (as they came to be known as) did not believe that the basic units in the grammar were words in their dictionary form. In one of the most famous examples, it was suggested that the semantic representation of the word *kill* was "cause + become + not + alive," and it was

assumed that these four items were semantic primitives. A series
of transformations would apply to produce the surface form in a
sentence such as *the farmer killed the duckling* from an underlying
form equivalent to "the farmer caused the duckling to become not
alive." Another example of this approach is the claim that the sentences *Seymour sliced the salami with a knife* and *Seymour used a
knife to slice the salami* had the same underlying form. That would
not be possible in the Chomskyan model, in which lexical items
(words) are basic units (Figure 3.3).

The farmer  CAUSED *the duckling* TO BECOME NOT *alive*
↓
The farmer  CAUSED *the duckling* TO BECOME *dead*
↓
The farmer  CAUSED *the duckling* to die
↓
The farmer killed the duckling

Figure 3.3    Diagram of generative semantics

In the period 1965–1975, there was a fierce debate between the
Interpretivists (as those belonging to the Chomsky school were
labeled) and the General Semanticists. The debate was bitter and at
times vicious. In an exchange of letters in 1973, James McCawley
wrote to Chomsky "the likelihood of either of us convincing the
other of anything is about zero" and Chomsky said in his reply
"everything you say ... is clearly wrong.... This is so plain and obvious that I am, frankly, startled that you don't see it." The disagreements were profound and, in the end, irrelevant. Chomsky routed
the Generative Semanticists, though he later went on to adopt
many of the notions he had contested earlier. The latter part of
this dispute was a sad period in the history of American linguistics
because gifted, well-meaning scholars who had started out from
much the same position and shared a common goal of describing
syntax ended up in bitterly opposed camps.

## The Chomskyan revolution: Phase three

### Types of rules

At this point, Chomsky began to move away from his original goal.
In *Syntactic Structures*, Chomsky defined a language as "a set

(finite or infinite) of sentences," and said that the grammar of the language should generate all the grammatical sentences of the language and none of the ungrammatical ones. As pointed out above, by "generate" he meant the mathematical sense of "specify the conditions for," and it was this notion that gave the label Generative Grammar to the approach Chomsky was advocating. At no time was the notion of generative grammar intended to suggest the actual production (i.e., utterance) of sentence, though there was sometimes confusion about this in popular accounts of Chomsky's ideas. By the time the conflict with the Generative Semanticists was over, Chomsky was no longer interested in generating all and only the sentences of any language. Instead, his attention had turned to notions of universal features of language, and as a result his analyses moved further away from the kind of structures that he had represented in *Syntactic Structures* and *Aspects of the Theory of Syntax* and also from the notion of a complete set of explicit rules for describing a language.

In the early days of generative grammar great importance was attached to the form of rules, partly because of the idea that the best description of a language would have the smallest possible set of economically expressed rules. That notion receded with a computational demonstration that any number of rules could (theoretically) be combined into one. It also should be said that the kind of notation Chomsky employed in *Syntactic Structures* made his rules look more rigorous than they actually were. In practice, it proved very difficult to present a comprehensive account of English syntax using the kind of transformational rules Chomsky had proposed, and there were few serious attempts to do so. Despite this problem, many people believed that Chomsky's approach was basically correct, though it needed refining. Nowadays nobody would attempt to write a grammar using the transformational rules of *Syntactic Structures* and *Aspects of the Theory of Syntax*, though there have been different versions of formal grammars using rules based on formal logic.

### I-language and E-language

More importantly, by the 1980s Chomsky's analysis no longer dealt with what most people consider language to be. Chomsky now drew a distinction between two senses of the word *language*. The first is what he called 'I-language' (internalized language), which is the organization of structures in the brain that underlies the comprehension and production of language. The second is what he called '**E-language**' (externalized language), which is what most people understand by the word *language*, namely a form of spoken and written communication. Chomsky believes that only I-language can be studied scientifically and his method remains one of constructing a model based on inferences from subjective judgments about sentences that are asserted to be part of the language. It has been pointed out that his model of I-language is based primarily on syntax, and thus ignores the other aspects of language. There is no direct evidence for the structure of this model, so it is hardly surprising that its shape has changed in fundamental and unpredictable ways over the past fifty years. Some of those who study I-language are optimistic that improved methods of exploring the functioning of the brain will help to support their analysis but others are more skeptical. It remains unclear whether the descriptions of I-language are intended to reflect psychological processes, but some claims seem to imply this.

## Universal Grammar (UG)

It is not necessary to follow in detail the changes in Chomsky's thinking over the years, since he has discarded much of the apparatus that he set up in the period from 1970 to the mid-1990s. His aim has been to move away from rules for language specific structures to more general principles as part of what Chomsky was now calling Universal Grammar (UG). Chomsky had always been interested in linguistic universals and in the innate component of a child's ability to learn a language. His aim was now to identify those features of UG that characterize all languages. Among these principles he included the way in which, to take one example, reflexive pronouns are dependent on another noun phrase, a notion that he called "binding." For example, we can say *John excused himself* because *himself* refers to John, but it is ungrammatical to say *\*John excused yourself* or *\*John excused themselves*, while in *John excused him* the pronoun *him* must refer to someone other than John. The use of a reflexive pronoun such as *himself* generally requires an antecedent referring to that individual in the same sentence, and there are complicated explanations of this situation, particularly in complex sentences.

Chomsky also used the example of case assignment to illustrate the notion of what he called "government." In English, only pronouns have overtly marked case, as in *I hit him*, where *I* is in the subject form and *him* in the object form, because a transitive verb such as *hit* assigns case to the subject and object respectively. The theory at this point came to be known as Government and Binding, and there are many other aspects of it that will not be mentioned here, partly because they would require a very technical explanation and partly because a new version was being developed.

## Principles and parameters

In what later came to be known as the Principles and **Parameters** model, in addition to the universal principles of UG which are claimed to be innate, there were identified clusters of variations from these general principles. These systematic exceptions were labeled "parameters," to refer to processes that operate in some languages and not in others. An example of a parameter that is often cited is the fact that in Italian it is not necessary in certain situations to have a pronoun subject for a verb, in contrast to English where any finite verb must have an overt subject. In Italian, the sentence *ho travato il libro*, literally "have found the book," is perfectly grammatical with the first person singular pronoun implied by the verb form *ho*. In English, with no indication of person or number indicated by the verb it is necessary to specify the pronoun and say *I have found the book*. The possibility for languages such as Italian to omit the pronoun is called "pro-drop" and this is an example of a parameter. There are other syntactic properties that are found in languages such as Italian that permit the omission of the pronoun (pro-drop) and together these properties form the parameter. Languages that do not allow pro-drop do not allow these other properties either. The Chomskyan notion of a parameter is that a child learning English or Italian does not need to notice this group of properties individually but simply needs to realize, for example, that the language is or is not pro-drop, and the other properties will follow. The Principles and

Parameters model thus concentrated on two notions: (1) universal principles common to all languages and (2) bundles of syntactic features (parameters) that are found in individual languages or families of languages, but not universally. Some of the attraction of this notion began to weaken when it appeared that a rather large number of parameters might need to be specified for each separate language. Moreover, it has been argued that some of the parameters would be difficult for any child to learn on the basis of the utterances heard. Not many linguists are still trying to identify parameters.

## The Chomskyan revolution: Phase four

The progress from *Syntactic Structures* to the Principles and Parameters model was a constant move from particular features of language to more general claims. In the course of this progression the notion of rules and constituents also changed. In his latest model, which Chomsky calls **The Minimalist Program**, there are no longer any constituents or rules. Instead, there is a random generating process that takes fully specified lexical items and combines them to make sentences. If the result satisfies certain conditions, the sentence can be interpreted for its meaning at the level of **Logical Form** and for its pronunciation at the level of **Phonetic Form**. If the combination of items does not produce an acceptable sentence, the process is said to have "crashed." This is a radical change from Chomsky's earlier work, and it has upset some of his former followers.

In the course of fifty years, Chomsky has come a long way from the aim of generating all the grammatical sentences of a language (and no ungrammatical ones) to an attempt to understand the nature of what he now calls the human language faculty. In this progress he has also moved away from the method of presenting a coherent set of rules that can specify the structure of a language through an algorithm for their application. Instead, he is trying to establish how the syntax of human languages can come close to being a "perfect system" for relating sound to meaning.

Chomsky's early work explored what the Czech linguist Mathesius called "the possibility of deeper and more hidden reality, lying at the root of the perplexing variety of outward phenomena." As he probed deeper and deeper into that hidden reality, Chomsky depended more and more on complex arguments rather than on supporting linguistic data, and he excluded more and more of the aspects of language that caused problems for his theories. There are still many linguists who believe that the emperor has splendid clothes, but many others have difficulty in seeing the garments. It is probably fair to say that the jury remains out on Chomsky's claims about linguistic structure, but one thing is undeniable. He has had an immense impact on the field and much more is known about the syntactic structure of human language as the result of his influence.

Chomsky's ideas and approaches enjoyed a great deal of success among his fellow linguists, particularly in the earlier stages, but they have not been accepted by all linguists who are interested in syntax. In addition to the Generative Semanticists, who shared the same general goals as Chomsky but differed in how to achieve those goals, there are many syntacticians who approach the topic from a very different perspective. Chomsky's approach has always been to describe the language faculty in isolation from its use. In particular, he has argued for the autonomy of syntax. Chomsky did not wish to deal with the messy aspects of language that occur when language is used in actual communication.

Chomsky drew a distinction between what he called the speaker's **linguistic competence** (or tacit knowledge of the language) and the use of that knowledge in what he called **linguistic performance**. His aim was always to describe competence, and his model does not convert easily to description of performance. Part of the reason is because of his use of abstract features that have no manifestation in the actual production of speech. There are other linguists who believe that it is possible to develop a formal model of syntax that is based instead on the surface order of language. These linguists have developed several versions of what are known as **Phrase Structure Grammars**. Chomsky had argued in *Syntactic Structures* that Phrase Structure Grammars were inadequate for the description of natural languages, but there are now several models that claim to have refuted this claim. They are too complex to summarize here but their advocates point out that their models are more compatible with what is known of actual speech production and perception. None of the models, however, has gained the popular attention that Chomsky's work has received.

## The counter-revolution: Phase two
## Functionalism

In contrast to Chomsky, there are many linguists who believe that you cannot understand language by treating it solely as an abstract system. They believe that the structure of language is affected by the ways in which it is used, by how the brain processes information, and by the purposes for which language is used. Many of those linguists who study language form in use have come to be known as Functionalists, in contrast to those like Chomsky who take a more abstract view and are sometimes labeled Formalists. As is generally the case with such labels, there are many variations within each category.

The functionalists disagree with generative grammarians of the Chomskyan type on a number of grounds. They believe that language is a social-cultural activity and that linguistic structure serves a cognitive and communicative function. The functionalists believe that linguistic structures are not arbitrary but are motivated by their function. One example is the preferred order of conjoined expressions (Table 3.1).

The functionalists believe that it is essential to investigate language structure by examining how people actually use language, an approach that Chomsky explicitly rejected. He believed that

Table 3.1   Preferred word order of conjoined expressions

| Preferred order | Less preferred order |
| --- | --- |
| **Near > far** | |
| now and then | then and now |
| here and there | there and here |
| **Adult > young** | |
| father and son | son and father |
| mother and daughter | daughter and mother |
| **Singular > plural** | |
| ham and eggs | eggs and ham |
| hammer and nails | nails and hammer |
| **Positive > negative** | |
| more or less | less or more |
| plus or minus | minus or plus |

any theory of grammatical structures had to be based on model of linguistic competence rather than on how speakers actually use language. In a famous statement, Chomsky set out his position: "Linguistic theory is concerned primarily with an ideal speaker-listener, in a completely homogeneous speech-community." This ideal-speaker listener would also not be troubled by such things as memory limitations, or distractions in using language. Since there are no ideal speaker-listeners to observe, the empirical basis for such a theory becomes a problem. This position is the polar opposite of the approach adopted by the functionalists.

## Grammaticality judgments

The method that Chomsky and his followers employed to investigate the system that such an ideal speaker-listener would have developed is the use of intuitive judgments about the grammaticality of possible sentences. In practice, the linguist generally used himself or herself as a source of information about what a proficient speaker-listener knows of the language. By claiming that certain sentences were grammatical and others ungrammatical, the linguist had grounds for arguing for or against a hypothesis about syntactic structure. Typically, these sentences were invented by the linguist in order to support (or reject) certain claims about syntactic structure. Functionalists (and others) have complained that many of these invented examples would never occur in any normal use of language, and consequently any system based on such examples does not reflect the ability of actual (as opposed to ideal) speaker-listeners to communicate through language. A few examples from Chomsky's works will illustrate the point. They are cited by Chomsky as examples of grammatical constructions that need to be accounted for in the grammar of English, but few people will recognize them as possible English sentences.

a. John is too stubborn to expect anyone to talk to

b. I wonder who the men expected to see each other

c. what did you wonder how to do?

d. who do the police think that the FBI discovered that Bill shot?

Instead of basing arguments on such invented (and implausible) examples such as these, Functionalists believe that it is better to base a description of language on the way people speak. A functionalist description does not assume that 'memory limitations' are 'grammatically irrelevant.' One formalist work states "If a speaker were to come along who could produce and understand million-word sentences of English, we would not say that that person spoke a different language from our own." No functionalist would make such a statement. On the contrary, the functionalists would point out that utterances are "chunked" into relatively short sequences, a fact that makes them easier to produce and to understand. Anyone who has listened to a lecture where the speaker is reading from a text that was designed for silent reading will know that it is often hard to follow what is being said. In contrast, everyday conversation is so easy for the listener to understand that there is seldom any sense of strain. Both speakers and listeners process language in relatively small sequences, usually no more than five to six words (see Chapter 4).

## Sentence grammars and utterance grammars

There is another fundamental difference between the Formalists and the Functionalists. Generative grammarians have followed Chomsky's early example of writing sentence grammars, that is, formal accounts of the structures underlying all the possible sentences in a language. However, the sentence is not a well-defined or necessary concept in spoken language (see Chapter 4) and the emphasis of generative grammarians on taking sentences as the basic units of grammar has had many unfortunate consequences. To take an obvious example, generative grammarians devoted a great deal of attention to the conditions under which personal pronouns such as *he* and *she* can be used within a single orthographic sentence with reference to an antecedent, but this use of pronouns constitutes only a minority of the uses of pronouns in speech. In conversation, the reference for most pronouns is found in the context of other utterances.

There are many other important differences between written and spoken language (Chapter 7). One is that complex subordinate clauses are much less common in speech. Another is that the syntactic structure of even simple sentences is different in speech. It turns out that even sentences of the kind *the boy hit the ball* are comparatively rare in speech. Much more common are sentences of the form *the boy hit it* and *he hit the ball*, or *he hit it*; that is, in speech it is much rarer to have two fully expressed noun phrases such as *the boy* and *the ball* in the same sentence. Part of the explanation for this is undoubtedly economy. In ordinary conversation the speaker does not need to spell out things that the listener already knows.

In their account of language, Functionalists pay attention to how language is processed by both speaker and listener. One example is the functionalist concern about the role of notions such as **subject** and **topic** in the use of language. In a formalist approach the notion of subject is defined by the position of a Noun Phrase relative to a verb, and the main role of the subject in the formalist model is to assign agreement of the verb. For example, in the sentence *the boy* was *hitting the ball*, the subject is *the boy* and this singular subject determines the form of the auxiliary *was*, in contrast to the sentence *the boys were hitting the ball* where the plural subject *the boys* requires the auxiliary *were*. In defining the notion of subject solely on the basis of position, there is no mention of what other role the subject plays in relation to the verb.

In an early form of functional grammar, Charles Fillmore pointed out that the grammatical notion of subject could have different roles. Functionalists are interested in the function served by the grammatical subject and include this information in the analysis. For example, in the sentence *the boy broke the window with a hammer*, there are three different functional roles, each of which can occur as subject.

a. the boy broke the window     (the boy = agent)

b. the window broke     (the window = recipient of the action)

c. the hammer broke
the window     (the hammer = instrument)

Fillmore labeled these functional roles **cases**, for example, agentive, instrumental, and so on and created a new model that he called **Case Grammar**. The three examples above can be represented by an underlying structure that is very different from the phrase structure trees used in the Chomskyan framework.

| VERB | RECIPIENT | INSTRUMENT | AGENT |
|------|-----------|------------|-------|
| ↓ | ↓ | ↓ | ↓ |
| break | the window | the hammer | the boy |

In his earlier work, Chomsky did not include information about case functions (though he later incorporated it as what he called **theta-marking**).

Functionalists are interested not only in the function of subjects but also in the notion of **topic**. The topic is what the speaker is talking about, and connected discourse shows how a topic is sustained or changed (see the example of conversation in Chapter 4). Tracking topic continuity and change in this way provides functionalists ways of analyzing how language is being used in communication. There is little interest in such matters in the formalist approach because it deals only with isolated sentences.

## The counter-revolution: Phase three Construction Grammars

Another difference between functionalists and formalists that has emerged in recent years is the nature of the basic building blocks for syntax. Formalist models, from *Syntactic Structures* on, have taken it for granted that syntax provides the structure for combining individual lexical items (words) into larger structures. Some functionalists have taken a different approach. They believe that human beings do not always create utterances by combining single words into syntactic patterns. They point out that there are many fixed expressions (constructions) that have to be stored as units even though they contain more than one word, for example, *let alone*, *on the other hand*, *to coin a phrase*, and so on.

The constructionists believe that there are units of grammar that are larger than words, which are meaningful, but whose meaning is not predictable from the basic meaning of the words in the construction. One example is the **resultative** construction as in *he wiped the table clean*, where the result of the wiping is that the table is clean. The constructionists point out that this construction can be used with a wide variety of verbs.

a. *Sam painted the house blue*

b. *He talked himself hoarse*

c. *She drank herself silly*

d. *Pat kicked Bob black and blue*

e. *Mary slapped Peter awake*

These are like idiomatic expressions in that the verbs are being used in a way that goes beyond their basic meaning. Formalists have always been aware that idioms present a problem for a model that assumes that all expressions are produced by combining individual words. The hackneyed example of an idiom is *kick the bucket* in the sense of "die." It is clear that *kick* has to be treated as a regular verb that can take the forms *kicks* and *kicked*, but there are problems with the phrase in its idiomatic sense. In its literal sense of striking a physical object, it would be possible to say *what John did on his way out of the room was kick the bucket* as an alternative to *John kicked the bucket on his way out of the room*. But it is not possible to say *what John did when he was shot in the head was kick the bucket* as an alternative to *John was shot in the head and kicked the bucket*.

Idioms are only the most conspicuous examples of fixed phrases that speakers use. There are a great many multi-word expressions that form part of everyday speech. Functionalists claim that frequency of occurrence plays an important role in both language processing and language change (see Chapter 6), and that it also influences children's language development. Notions of frequency played no role in earlier formalist approaches because their grammars were not based on how language is used, but some syntacticians are combining a formal approach with attention to aspects of speech production and comprehension, including the influence of frequency and fixed expressions. A major disagreement with

Chomsky's approach for recent formalists is the rejection of hidden levels of syntax.

## Children's language development

Perhaps because they were usually focused on complex syntactic structures, formalists until recently have tended to pay little attention to multi-word expressions. This has had a profound influence on theories of the child's language development. Chomsky has argued in extremely strong terms that children could not possibly develop an adequate grammar on the basis of the kind of speech they are likely to hear. Consequently, he has argued for an innate capacity (**Universal Grammar**) that will make it possible for the child to acquire the complex system that he sees as underlying knowledge of a language.

Functionalists, on the other hand, have suggested that children develop their linguistic skills incrementally by taking patterns they have heard and extrapolating from them to new situations. Chomsky, in his review of B.F.Skinner's *Verbal Behavior* ridiculed the idea that children's language development was a process of imitation, refined by a process of rewards and punishments. Linguists studying children's language acquisition in the Chomskyan framework were able to show how many aspects of the children's early speech could not have been the result of imitation of adult models. However, functionalists believe that the swing of the pendulum against an extreme behaviorist view of language development went too far. Although there are features of child language that could not have been imitated from adults, there is plenty of evidence that children also expand patterns of expression based on adult models.

The claim for innate syntactic knowledge (Universal Grammar) followed inevitably from the notion of syntax as an autonomous component of language. If the syntactic component is independent of the meaningful aspects of communication, there is no way that a child (or anyone else) could learn language. Since, on this premise, it is impossible to learn the structural aspects of syntax, and since all normal children develop language skills, the Chomskyan claim is that they must be born with this ability. In fact, Chomsky refused to suggest any order in which children might develop their linguistic ability; instead, he chose to present his model as an idealization in which language acquisition is "instantaneous." It is unfortunate that popular accounts of Chomsky's claims about innate grammar do not draw attention to the counterfactual underpinnings of his position.

One of the arguments that Chomsky put forward in support of Universal Grammar was what he called "the poverty of the stimulus." By this he meant that children are not provided with the kind of negative examples that will enable them to learn that some kinds of sequences of words are wrong. In other words, adults are not always providing children with examples of ungrammatical sentences and telling them "Don't do this." Since nobody ever explains to children that certain constructions are ungrammatical, the claim is that the children must know in advance (through Universal Grammar) that they are not possible. However, the kinds of examples of ungrammatical sentences given as examples by formalists are often hard to imagine being uttered in any context. Here are a few examples. (The asterisk marks ungrammaticality)

> a. *who did Mary see John and?
> b. *what were you wondering which clothes to do?
> c. *who did you ask when left?
> d. *what do you remember where John read?

These are all actual examples given by formalists discussing syntactic structures. The models of syntax that they are advocating would correctly rule out such sentences while allowing other kinds of questions that are grammatical in the language. It may seem strange to many people that these linguists should have paid so much attention paid to things that could never be said, and so little attention to how language is actually used. This is possible only in an approach to language that (a) ignores the communication situation; (b) separates form from meaning; and (c) deals with individual sentences isolated from any context.

### Stasis vs. dynamism

The formalist approach to language treats it as a static, timeless system. This attitude goes back to Ferdinand de Saussure who wished to separate the study of a language from its historical development. He gave the example of a chess board. An onlooker examining the chess board at an advanced stage of the game does not know how the pieces reached their present location. Saussure's argument was based on the notion that the speakers of a language do not need to know the history of their language in order to be able to speak or understand it. This is clearly correct. Only those who have studied an earlier period of the English language will be able to explain why the past tense of *teach* is *taught* and not *\*teached* or why the plural of *mouse* is *mice* (see Chapter 6). This, however, does not mean that it is correct to analyze language as a static system.

Speech is a dynamic process and the form of language spoken in any community is never fixed once and for all time. Saussure's metaphor of the chess board is quite misleading. A better analogy for language would be a soccer game or basketball game, where the players are in constant motion and responding to the movements of other players. While much of the language spoken in a community does not change rapidly, there are always changes taking place. We learn new words or expressions and stop using others, and we may change how we pronounce certain forms. We also change how and where we use language. (A Rip Van Winkle asleep for the past thirty years would get a shock hearing some of the taboo language common in many films and television programmes nowadays.) Some functionalists have even argued that all grammar is "emergent" rather than a relatively fixed system that children learn.

The formalists who were developing an **algorithmic model** often emphasized the creativity of the language system. In fact, Steven Pinker went so far as to claim that "virtually every sentence that a person utters or understands is a brand-new combination of words, appearing for the first time in the history of the universe." This ignores the fact that communicative efficiency often depends upon routines that are familiar and can be processed rapidly. The pace of life would be much slower if people were constantly creating new ways of dealing with each other in everyday situations.

## Revolution and counter-revolution

The past fifty years have seen a remarkable number of studies of syntactic structure in a wide range of languages and as a result a great deal has been discovered about linguistic structure, language processing, language acquisition, and language disorders. As of the time of writing this account, no great synthesizer has appeared on the scene to summarize what has been achieved, sorting out the features of lasting value from the ephemeral, but there are now many areas of agreement among syntacticians, and much of the rancor that was manifest earlier seems to have dissipated. It will probably turn out that both formalists and functionalists have contributed to greater understanding of language, but at the present moment there is no consensus on what the contribution of either group would be. In syntax, as in every other aspect of human language, there is still plenty to be discovered.

It is easy to understand why linguists should be so concerned about syntax. Speech is a system of communicating by using sounds to convey meaning. As was shown in Chapter 2, the study of sound is carried out by investigators from a variety of disciplines, and linguists have no privileged status there. Chapter 1 showed that a similar situation exists with respect to meaning. The one domain in which linguists rule supreme and without competition from other disciplines is the structure of language, both syntax and morphology. Concentrating on these aspects has enabled linguists from a variety of theoretical orientations to discover a great deal about the world's languages, but looking at the form of language is only one way of approaching the subject. Other ways of looking at language will be examined in the chapters that follow.

## SUGGESTIONS FOR FURTHER READING

Noam Chomsky's *Syntactic Structures* still makes exciting reading even though its hopes and aspirations have not been realized. Of his later works, *Language and Problems of Knowledge* is probably the most accessible. There are many books about Chomsky, most of them are fairly technical and not easy for lay readers. Neil Smith's *Noam Chomsky: Ideas and Ideals* is very readable but his enthusiastic view of Chomsky is not shared by everybody. Christine Kenneally's *The First Word* is not primarily concerned with syntax, but her short chapter on Chomsky is as good a short account as anyone has written. Cedric Boeckx's *Language in Cognition* deals with Chomsky's work in the context of recent work on cognition.

Two good accounts of different approaches to syntax can be found in Frederick Newmeyer's *Generative Linguistics* and *Language Form and Language Function*. The latter gives a good account of the difference between the formal and the functional approaches, though biased in favor of the formalists. One functional view is presented in William Croft and D.Alan Cruse *Cognitive Linguistics*. T. Givón's *Functionalism and Grammar* provides a wide-ranging account of functional grammar in an impressive variety of languages. Kasper Boye and Elisabeth Engberg-Pedersen's *Language Usage and Language Structure* presents various recent approaches to the study of syntax. Michael A.K. Halliday's *Explorations in the Functions of Grammar* is an introduction to a very different functional approach, one that takes the social and cultural context into consideration.

Robert Stockwell, Paul Schachter, and Barbara Hall Partee's *The Major Syntactic Structures of English* presents a comprehensive account of English syntax in a Case Grammar framework. Adele Goldberg's *Constructions* is a good introduction to construction grammar. A more complete account can be found in Graeme Trousdale and Nikolas Gisborne's *Topics in English Linguistics: Constructional Approaches to English Grammar*. Other types of grammars are discussed in Peter Sells *Lectures on Contemporary Syntactic Theories*.

A critical account of Chomsky's changing syntactic models and a proposal for a more realistic approach to formal syntax (without hidden levels) is presented in Peter Culicover and Ray Jackendoff's *Simpler Syntax*. Peter Seuren launches a powerful attack on minimalism in *Chomsky's Minimalism*. William Snyder's *Child Language* gives an example of a Chomskyan approach to the study of children's language development, but it is not easy to follow. The history of the earlier period is described in Peter Matthews *Grammatical Theory in the United States from Bloomfield to Chomsky*. The debate between Chomsky and the Generative Semanticists is examined (from an anti-Chomsky perspective) by Geoffrey Huck and John Goldsmith *Ideology and Linguistic Theory*.

Michael Devitt's *Ignorance of Language* challenges the view that Chomsky's structures are psychologically real. John Hawkins demonstrates how psychological processes affect linguistic structure in *Efficiency and Complexity in Grammars*. Katharina Hartmann's *Right Node Raising and Gapping* shows the influence of prosody on grammatical structures. Jim Miller and Regina Weinert examine the difference between spoken and written syntax in *Spontaneous Spoken Language*. In *Language Misconceived*, Karol Janicki argues that much theoretical linguistics suffers from taking an essentialist perspective of language. Anyone interested in the actual syntax of English rather than

theories about it will find much information in the accessible comprehensive survey of English grammar provided by James McCawley in *The
Syntactic Phenomena of English* and in *A Comprehensive Grammar
of the English Language* by Randolph Quirk, Sidney Greenbaum,
Geoffrey Leech, and Jan Svartvik.

# 4

# Language as Communication

Just as it is possible for physicists to think of light as particle or wave, in a somewhat parallel fashion, linguists can approach language as form or interaction. The previous three chapters have considered aspects of language that can be examined from a formal perspective. The present chapter requires a radically different method of investigation. Formal linguists (Chapter 3) and philosophers (Chapter 1) have tended to carry out their investigations from an armchair (or perhaps desk chair) perspective, relying on their access to their own knowledge of language. Phoneticians (Chapter 2) have largely carried out their analysis in the laboratory, in many cases limiting their examples to the pronunciation of single (often short) words. Of course, linguists and phoneticians also collect examples of language in many parts of the world, but they have generally concentrated on eliciting isolated examples of linguistic forms rather than focusing on how these forms are used interactively in the community. To put it another way, such investigators have usually recorded monologists providing direct answers to specific questions. Using such methods, linguists and anthropologists have recorded priceless information about many languages that have since disappeared or are likely to do so shortly. There was no alternative to this method until relatively recently because all the forms had to be transcribed by the researcher at the time they were elicited. The development of the portable tape recorder has transformed this situation. It is now possible not only to make recordings to be transcribed at a later date, it is also possible to record people speaking to each other in a variety of situations (see Chapter 5). The possibility of recording actual interactions does not solve all the problems but it allows investigators to study people talking to each other in ways that would have been difficult (and often impossible) to do before the availability of portable tape recorders. This development makes it possible to investigate language as a dynamic process.

## Spoken language

Here is an extract from a conversation between two Scottish working-class women:

(Glasgow working-class women)

| | | |
|---|---|---:|
| Mary: | but then we heard | 1 |
| | it was for anybody | 2 |
| | that any women could join it | 3 |
| Betty: | that's right | 4 |
| Mary: | so we came here | 5 |
| Betty: | aye | 6 |
| Mary: | and then we found | 7 |
| | that we could do classes | 8 |
| Betty: | aye | 9 |
| | which is excellent | 10 |
| Mary: | so I done my first aid course | 11 |
| | in here twice | 12 |
| | passed it | 13 |
| Betty: | did you? | 14 |
| Mary: | aye | 15 |
| Betty: | excellent | 16 |
| Mary: | passed it | 17 |
| | and then we done– | 18 |
| | we did wee mosaic things | 19 |
| | in here as well | 20 |
| | but then we done that personal–eh– | 21 |
| Betty: | personal presentation | 22 |
| Mary: | aye | 23 |
| | we done that | 24 |

The first thing to note is that this is very different from written prose, such as the kind of language used in this book and many other types of printed works. This illustrates some of the differences between spoken language and written language (see Chapter 7).

There are many utterances in this extract that are not sentences, for example, *which is excellent, passed it, excellent,* but they are the kinds of utterances that are common in everyday conversation. In order to understand how human beings use language to communicate it is necessary to examine how people speak. This is very different from the attempts to model abstract syntactic structures based on intuitive grammaticality judgments in the ways described in Chapter 3.

Chomsky pointed out that a recording of natural speech would display such things as **false starts** (as in line 18) and argued that this would make it more difficult for a child learning the syntax of the language. Recent researchers into children's language learning have pointed out that most speech directed toward children does not in fact have problems that would complicate the child's understanding of what was said. The functionalists argue that the kind of language that generative grammarians have investigated on the basis of intuitive grammaticality judgments is written language, not speech (see Chapter 7), and children learn to speak before they learn to read and write. In line 13 Mary does not need to repeat the phrase *my first aid course* because her listener will be able to recognize what *it* refers to. Nor does Mary need to supply the subject *I* in the utterance *passed it,* since that is obvious from the context. English is not a pro-drop language in Chomskyan terms (see Chapter 3) but examples like line 13 where there is no subject to the verb are very common in conversation.

The excerpt from the conversation begins with a reference that cannot be retrieved from the context: *then we heard that it was for everybody.* There is no way to know from this remark what the speaker is talking about, which was the Women's Centre, where the recording was made. Before the extract begins, Mary had said that she had thought the Women's Centre had only been for "battered wives" or people like that. The use of the pronoun *it* to refer to the Women's Centre marks it as **old information**, something that the hearer would already know about. The topic is continued in *that any women could join it,* where *it* again refers to the Women's Centre. The reference is continued in *so we came* *here*, where *here* also refers to the Women's Centre. The topic changes at line 7, *and then we found that we could do classes*, where a new topic is introduced with the full noun *classes*. This topic is elaborated by the later remark *so I done my first aid course*, (*done* is frequently used as the past tense of *do* by some Scottish speakers) with the **new information** provided by the noun phrase *my first aid course*, referred to again in lines 13 and 19 by the pronoun *it*, since it is no longer new information. Two new pieces of information are introduced, *wee mosaic things* in line 19 and *personal presentation* in lines 21–22 (with a little help from the listener). The latter is then referred to in line 24 by the pronoun *that*. The example thus illustrates how people use language when they are talking with each other, introducing new topics with nouns but using pronouns to refer to things that have already been mentioned.

## Conversation

> To hear perfectly and answer precisely are the great perfections of conversation. (Duc de la Rochefoucault)

Almost everywhere you go, you will come across groups of people engaged in conversation. This is something that we do without thinking of it as a great human achievement, but it is. Listening to a learned scholar presenting an erudite paper or to an eloquent preacher delivering a sermon or to a smooth-talking politician giving a speech we may be impressed by the quality of the language used, but what each of them is doing is actually much less complex than the everyday activity of conversing in a group. Participating in a conversation requires very rapid processing of speech both as a listener and as a speaker. We often become conscious of this when we try to participate in a conversation in a language that we know less well. Everyone seems to speak very quickly and by the time we have decided how to say something, the opportunity has gone. In our own language, we seldom experience these difficulties. The ways in which speakers interact have been studied under the label **Conversation Analysis.**

The Conversation Analysts have identified certain basic "rules" for conversation. Most of these are not rules that we have learned consciously, though some come into the category of good manners, as when we teach our children to say *please* and *thank you*. They are also not likely to be the subject of overt comment if you fail to follow the "rule," but your interlocutors may feel that there is something wrong. There is a general principle in all well-ordered vocal communication that two people should not talk at the same time. In certain formal situations, such as committee meetings or a court of law, a chairman or other official will regulate the proceedings. A similar rule operates informally in everyday conversation, though as will be shown below there are various exceptions to this rule. Occasionally, there may be an overlap between speakers (see below) but if two people persist in talking at the same time there is no longer a "conversation" but rather some kind of contest of the wills, as when a disagreement turns into a shouting match. In normal conversation, there is an orderly system of turn taking, with one person mainly listening until the speaker has finished before offering a response. In a two-party conversation the participants alternate in speaking, even if one person dominates the conversation. In a multi-party conversation, there may be competition for the floor and this requires paying particularly careful attention to what the speaker is saying.

## Turn-taking rules

In order to avoid interrupting the current speaker, participants have to time their contribution to coincide with the end of the speaker's turn. This requires two simultaneous mental activities. The first is to follow what the speaker is saying and at the same time to anticipate when the speaker's contribution is about to end. It is important to anticipate the end of the utterance because in a conversation with more than two people there will be only a split-second opportunity for you to offer your remark. If you are not ready, someone else may jump in before you get the chance. In order to be ready, however, you also have to have thought out what you want to say. So in any multi-party conversation you have to be listening carefully and processing what the speaker says so that you know when a possible entry point may occur, and at the same time you have to have prepared in your mind what you want to say. Even in a two-person conversation, you have to be ready because even a short silence on your part may give your interlocutor the impression that something is wrong. Sometimes a speaker gives an indication of being in trouble and the listener can jump in to supply a word or to complete a construction. When Mary hesitates *but then we done that personal – eh*, Betty supplies the missing word *personal presentation*.

There are various clues to indicate when the speaker's turn could end. One is the syntactic structure. Speakers are not likely to end in the middle of a construction that requires, for example, a verb or an object to be coherent. There are also intonational and rhythmic clues that the speaker is reaching a pausing place that might indicate the end of his/her turn. Occasionally, a listener will misjudge this and start to speak only to be told "Wait a minute – I haven't finished yet," but such situations are an exception because we are very skilful at turn-taking.

## Interruptions

There was an early study claiming to show that men were more likely to interrupt women than the other way round, and this view was widely disseminated as if it were established fact. Later more careful studies have shown that the situation is much more complicated and that not all overlaps between speakers should be interpreted as interruptions.

Another example illustrates this. Andrew is describing a place he had visited on a Scottish loch not far from Glasgow.

(Glasgow middle-class men)
Andrew: It's just, it's about two bumps in the road before Rowardennan
Bill: mmhm
Andrew: on the left. If you go up from Salachie Bay and you carry on, there's a place where you come to a little loch on the left, which is not Loch Lomond, it's called the Du Lochan, the black lochan
Bill: Oh I see yes, uh-huh.
Andrew: and it's immediately at the roadside. You go through the oak forest,
Bill: mmhm
Andrew: and up and down, up and down, it's like wee Trossachs type part.
Bill: Yes.

| | |
|---|---|
| Andrew: | And you come over crest down a hill and there's a track on the left with a gate, and you probably won't notice that but you would immediately notice there was very suddenly water on your left which rather looks like it might be a big inlet of Loch Lomond, but it's not. |
| Bill: | I see, uh-huh |

In this example, Bill regularly acknowledges that he has heard and understood what Andrew is telling him by saying *mhmm, uhuh, yes, I see*. Such contributions are called **Minimal Responses** because they do not add any new information but signal that the listener is following what has been said. Sometimes, Bill's responses come in the middle of Andrew's constructions but they do not interrupt the flow, because they are not assuming an independent turn. This is one of the cases where the rule that two people should not speak at once is violated. Minimal responses can occur anywhere without violating that principle, and they do not count as interruptions.

## Minimal responses

Minimal Responses such as *mmhm* and *uhuh* do not count as full turns in the conversation. They indicate that the listener is paying attention and following the story. Stories are quite a frequent occurrence in conversation and they give the narrator license to speak longer than a normal turn. The listener's role, however, is not simply a passive one; the listener has to reassure the narrator that there are no problems. Minimal responses, including forms such as *yes* and *right* and expressions such as *I see* and *I know*, perform this function.

## Adjacency pairs

One of the ways that the speaker can signal the end of a turn is by asking a direct question, since this is a way of requesting someone else to take over the role of talking. Questions belong to a category of speech acts that require a response. Conversation Analysts call such sequences as a question followed an answer **Adjacency Pairs**. Failure to respond at all indicates that something is very wrong, though in fact this is rare in conversation. There are many kinds of remarks in addition to questions that require an immediate response. A greeting demands a response; a request requires either an acceptance or a rejection; an invitation requires an acceptance or a refusal; a compliment requires some kind of acknowledgement; an accusation requires an admission or a denial; a stated opinion requires a response that indicates agreement or disagreement, or some indication of a reluctance to offer either. "Requires" in these instances simply means that the speaker will sense a problem if the expected response is not forthcoming. It is usually difficult to notice that something has NOT happened in a conversation, but the failure to respond to the first part of an Adjacency Pair can sometimes be dramatically obvious, and in certain cases insulting. There are other situations in which silence may be used deliberately.

## Speed of response

More frequently the sign of a problem is a noticeable pause before the response is given. The pause can be very short, little over a fifth of a second, and still signify a problem. If someone says to you "Would you like to go out tonight?" a hesitation of more than a fifth of a second may signal to the inviter that you are unsure whether you want to go or not. A prompt acceptance will reassure the speaker that you genuinely want to go. A quick response explaining why you cannot go will not disrupt the conversation. A delayed response, however, may indicate some uncertainty on your part. There may be a variety of reasons why you are hesitating. You may not want to go and are trying to think of a polite way to turn down the invitation. You may be unsure what the invitation really means. You may have alternative plans that would have to be scrapped and you are wondering whether you can do this or whether you want do this. Whatever the reason for your delay in responding, the inviter will interpret this delay as a problem. The speaker may then add something intended to reassure you or to make the invitation more attractive, mentioning a new restaurant, or a friend who will join you, or a film that you could see. Again, this elaboration of the invitation will occur a split-second after your hesitation has been noted. Alternatively, the speaker may withdraw the invitation rather than risk a face-threatening rejection. In general, many of the "rules" of conversation contribute to minimizing awkwardness in the situation.

## Discourse markers

For example, if you know immediately that you do not want to go, you are unlikely simply to say "No" or even "No thanks." Such an abrupt rejection is likely to be perceived as rude. Generally, you will try to find a way to soften the negative impact of rejecting the invitation. In many cases you may begin your response with the little word *well*, as in "Well, I've got this report to prepare by tomorrow" or "Well, Joan's brother said he might be dropping in tonight." Neither of these responses precludes a decision to accept the invitation but they prepare the ground for a gentle rejection, if you should decide against. Beginning your response with the word *well* immediately signals that you are not going to give a quick acceptance. We often use *well* when not giving the specific response that a question asks. For example, when Mary was asked the question "How long have you been in there?" the response she gave was "Well I was pregnant when I moved in there." Since she had been talking about her daughter and mentioned her age, the response was informative, though it was not in the simplest form "Fifteen years." *Well* is a good example of a so-called Discourse Marker that does not have a simple paraphrasable meaning in this function. (There are two other words *well*. One is the adverb as in *He is doing well*. The other is the noun as in *going to the well too often*. Neither of these meanings is relevant to the discourse marker *well*.) Discourse markers, as their name suggests, help to guide the listener as to how to interpret the utterance, but it is no use looking in the dictionary or grammar books for guidance on how to use or understand discourse markers.

Another frequently used discourse marker is the little word *oh*. This can be used to introduce a signal that one has understood what has been said, as in the following example.

(Glasgow middle-class women)
    Alison:   Yes. (laughing) Everything's from Argos 'cause there's no other shops where he is
    Meg:    (laughing) Oh I see

     *Oh* can also be used at the start of a signal of agreement:
(Glasgow middle-class women)
    Alison:  it's a fascinating library
    Meg:    oh yes

Well is also used in this way:
(Glasgow middle-class women)
    Alison:   it's like your own house isn't it?
    Meg:      well that's right

*Oh* is also used in expressions of emotion such as *oh dear* or *oh wonderful*, and many expletives, or in comments such as *oh I could strangle her.* Another use is to introduce questions, checking on a situation, such as *oh were you there?* And *oh does she?*

Both *well* and *oh* are often used when people are reporting what someone has thought or said:

(Glasgow middle-class women)
    Alison:   I said "Well maybe it's in the fridge Elizabeth"
    Meg:      and I thought "Oh this'll be no problem"

When speakers are telling a story, they often quote what someone else had said, apparently repeating the actual wording (see below). The quoted dialogue is often introduced by a verb such as *say,* and usually the intonation signals when the dialogue begins, but discourse markers such as *oh* and *well* help to indicate when the quoted speech begins.

Discourse markers, such as *well* and *oh*, have the function of guiding the listener's comprehension of an utterance. They make it easier for the listener to process the message, but they do not usually feature in philosophers' study of meaning. Other discourse markers include expressions such as *you know, you see, I mean,* and the new "redundant" item popular among younger speakers *like.* These expressions are often deplored by those who consider them an example of slovenly speech, but like most aspects of language that survive obloquy, they serve a useful function.

## Breath groups

As was pointed out earlier (in Chapter 3), people do not speak in the kind of long sentences that can be found in writing (see also Chapter 7). Instead, speakers utter their remarks in "chunks" (or breath groups) of about five words. These chunks are often not complete syntactic constructions but the rhythm and intonation guide the listener to the connection between chunks. Discourse markers such as *you know* and *I mean* often help in this "chunking" in a variety of ways. For example, contrary to the apparent implication of shared meaning, *you know* is sometimes used in initial position to introduce new information:

(Glasgow middle-class women)
    Meg:    you know I had mentioned the fact that I had taught for a few
           years
    Alison:  you know there was a violent thunderstorm

This use of *you know* as a discourse marker is quite different from the meaning that the words have when used literally. In this case, the listener did *not* know the information that was about to be communicated; on the contrary, it was new information that the speaker was providing. Consulting the dictionary would again not help in understanding how the words are being used in this expression. *You know* is also sometimes used before an elaboration intended to clarify what the speaker has just said:

(Glasgow middle-class women)
    Sarah: it's just horrendous you know – absolute madness
    Meg:  there's a lot of pressure you know – power stuff– in the pack

At other times, the use of *you know* occurs at a place where the speaker has completed a syntactic unit and the listener has an opportunity to respond:

(Glasgow middle-class women)
    Jean:   I'd got caught on the phone          1
       by somebody who was asking for help you know  2
    Fiona: mmhm      3
    Jean:   and I came out thinking "This is ridiculous" you know  4
       "she's wanting help  5
       and yet my son's the one who's being left at home" you know  6

In this example, speaker Jean is telling a story and Fiona's only contribution is *mmhm* at line 3. The use of *you know* at the end of line 2 signals the end of a construction. At this point, speaker Fiona could have made a comment or asked a question but she limits herself to this minimal response, which allows her to show that she is following what has been said. Discourse markers such as *you know* and *I mean* help to organize speech and make it easier to follow.

# Telephone conversations

Minimal responses are particularly important during telephone conversations, because the speakers cannot see each other. In face-to-face conversations, the listener can show by eye-contact, facial expressions, nods, and other visual signals that the message is being attended to. These are not available on the telephone, so the speaker must rely on the listener's vocal responses. If you say nothing, the person speaking to you may think the connection has been lost and say "Are you still there?"

Telephone conversations have been studied in some detail because they remove the complications of the physical context (see below) of face-to-face interaction. Telephone conversations are usually between two people, and they have the advantage that they can be recorded very easily. There is, however, one unusual aspect to telephone conversations: the person who is initiating the conversation does not speak first. When the telephone rings the person who answers speaks first, generally before knowing who is calling. This gives the caller a distinct advantage. If the person who answers the phone is someone you do not want to speak to, you can simply terminate the call. (We have all seen this often in television dramas where a lover does not want to speak to the spouse, or reveal who is calling.) In most cases, however, the caller will proceed to identify himself/herself or to ask to speak to someone. In many cases, it is not necessary to check on anyone's identity because we can often immediately recognize a friend's voice, which is another sign of the rapid processing of information that occurs in spoken situations. There are also various routines that follow familiar patterns, as in this invented example:

[Telephone rings in an office]
    A:  Hello
    B:  Is Mr. Simpson there?
    A:  Yes, would you like to speak to him?
    B:  Please
    A:  Can I say who's calling?
    B:  Peter Thompson from Liberty Travel

There are, of course, many different routines for beginning telephone conversations and variations on each but they take place within a framework of expectations about how to begin and respond to a telephone call. There are also certain expectations about how to end a telephone call. The least cooperative is simply to hang up without saying anything, as again frequently occurs in soap operas and other dramas, when a character wishes to express anger or some other such emotion. Simply saying "Goodbye" without any warning will in most cases be interpreted as a sign of little consideration for the other person's feelings, as may happen when a supervisor is ending a conversation with an employee. In most cases of friendly telephone conversations, however, there will occur a kind of ritual dance in preparation to terminating the call. When we are in face-to-face conversation, there are many ways in which we can signal that we are about to put an end to the conversation. We can stand up, or push our chair back, or put our papers in a briefcase, and so on. There are many visual signals that prepare the ground for parting remarks, such as "Well, that's all we've got time for," "I'll see you next week" or "Give my best wishes to Helen." All of these are preliminaries to the actual leave-taking. On the telephone this slow separation must be done verbally, as illustrated in another invented example:

A:  Well it's been nice talking to you
B:  I was glad to hear all your news
A:  Give the kids a hug from me
B:  Sure
A:  Talk to you again soon
B:  You bet
A:  Bye
B:  Bye

## The context of communication

Telephone conversations, as pointed out earlier, provide a useful way of isolating oral communication from the physical context of face-to-face interaction, but it is the latter situation that is more important. The anthropological linguist Dell Hymes once proposed the acronym SPEAKING to summarize the various aspects of linguistic communication. The mnemonic is set out below in Table 4.1.

### Setting and scene

Hymes' acronym may seem like overkill but it simply draws attention to the complex factors that affect our speech (or writing), though they are so commonplace that we usually take them for

Table 4.1   Dell Hymes' SPEAKING acronym

---

S is the **Setting**, that is, the physical circumstances, including the time and place of the speech event. It is also the **Scene** or subjective definition of the occasion.

P refers to the **Participants**, those taking part in the event.

E refers to **Ends**, meaning the aims of the event. Hymes distinguishes between the goals of the individual participants and the overall purpose of the interaction.

A stands for **Act** sequence, which less obviously means the message form and content of the message.

K stands for **Key**, or the tone, manner, and spirit in which the communication is carried out.

I stands for **Instrumentalities**, by which Hymes meant the form of language used, including the distinction between spoken and written language.

N refers to **norms of interaction**, not only how people behave but also how they evaluate other people's behavior.

G stands for **genres**, such as conversation, storytelling, lecturing, reciting, and so on.

---

granted without thinking about them. Take the notion of Setting, for example. We all know that where an event takes place affects the way in which we speak. We have to adjust the volume of our voices to noisy or quiet conditions, and to distance (by shouting or whispering). The tone of a committee meeting may be different if held in a formal board room or in a restaurant. Different forms of speech are appropriate in church or at a sporting event. It is not only the physical setting that affects how we speak. The notion of Scene refers to the character of the event. A group sitting round a table may be holding a committee meeting or eating dinner and the kind of language used will be affected by which it is. There is also the possibility of different perceptions of the event by the participants. What someone intended as a casual conversation may be perceived by the interlocutor as an interrogation or an interview.

**Participants**

Much more salient in any speech event is the relationship of the participants. There is an obvious difference when we are among friends or strangers. Even more important are the status roles: older/

younger, employer/employee, parent/child, and so on. One of the obvious ways in which a difference in status may affect speech is in the use of address terms. An employer may address an employee using first name but expect to be addressed as Mr. Smith. In many languages there is a difference in the pronouns used, depending upon status and familiarity. In French, for example, to express the notion "you are the teacher" it is necessary to choose between the form *vous êtes le professeur,* which shows more respect (or distance) and *tu es le professeur,* which is more likely to be used by a friend or someone who is in a higher status. At an earlier time, there was a similar distinction between *you* and *thou* in English, but the situation changed in the 17th century (with some assistance from Quakers who refused to distinguish the rank of the addressee). There are languages such as Japanese and Javanese that have several degrees of respect in the forms of address and it is always necessary to employ the form that is appropriate for you as a speaker in relation to the status the person you are addressing. Regardless of the formal distinctions found in any language, the relationship between the speakers will affect the form of speech. There is no neutral form of speech.

There is also the phenomenon known as **Speech Accommodation**. In certain kinds of situation one of the participants may adjust his or her form of speech to be more similar to that of the other speaker. This can happen in formal situations where a subordinate addressing his or her superior may be careful not to use the slang or taboo expressions frequently employed when speaking with friends. Similarly, when two speakers come from different social milieus either may choose to adopt a form of speech closer to that of the other. For example, a manager may use informal expressions in talking with a worker, with the intention of minimizing the distance in rank. Conversely, the worker may use more a rather formal style when seeking to impress a boss. Any difference in status, age, gender or ethnicity can trigger speech accommodation. This complicates the situation for those who wish to investigate differences in speech (see Chapter 5).

It is not only the participants in the sense of those who are involved in the conversation who influence the form of speech. Uninvolved "overhearers" can also affect the situation. Most adolescents will have had the uncomfortable experience of trying to talk to a close friend in the presence of a parent or teacher or some other adult, who may or may not be listening. The conversation in such circumstances is likely to be constrained in a number of ways, including avoiding the use of slang and taboo expressions, which would not be the case if there were no adults within earshot. Similar kinds of constraints apply to adult participants in a wide variety of situations, including talking on the telephone in the presence of someone your caller wants to talk about.

## Ends

Hymes' term Ends was obviously chosen to suit the acronym and covers two separate notions. The first concerns the goals of the individual speakers. The second is the purpose of the interaction. This distinction can best be seen in a dispute mediation session, where each side has its own objectives, which are not necessarily compatible, but where the overall goal is to accomplish some agreement. Of course, most conversations are not so obviously antagonistic but even in friendly exchanges there is often competition for the floor and some participants may feel that they have not had the opportunity to make their views known. There can be many individual goals for speakers that may or may not be transparent: angling for an invitation or a loan, raising the possibility of getting a job, and, of course, attempts at seduction. Whatever the motivation for the speaker, it will have an effect on the form of speech. Even if the goal is simply to have a pleasant, relaxing conversation with a friend, there will be some forms of speech that will be more appropriate than others.

## Act of speech (form and content)

In Hymes' model, the A refers to Act sequence, by which he meant the message form and the content of the message. By this he apparently means those aspects of the utterance that could be described in the framework of formal linguistics (see Chapters 1 and 3). He drew a distinction between form and content by referring to a situation where someone is reporting what another person said. One way is to repeat what the other person said: *Peter said to me "I'm buying a Mercedes."* The other way is to use what is called reported speech: *Peter told me that he was buying a Mercedes.* The latter form reports only the content of what Peter said; the former reports both form and content.

The essential point, however, is that the speakers need to share the ability to determine the message content from the message form. In other words, they need to be speaking the same language. On the other hand, there are communities in which people regularly speak more than one language, and frequently speakers will switch from one language to another, even in the middle of an utterance. This process, known as **code-switching**, used to be taken as a sign that the speakers imperfectly controlled either or both languages. This turns out to be a misjudgment. In many cases, speakers who are fully fluent in both languages will switch back and forth for a variety of reasons, often connected to topic or attitude (see Chapter 5). Code-switching is one example that fits into the next item on Hymes' list.

## Key

Key refers to the tone, manner and spirit in which the communication is carried out. This is a way of referring to stylistic differences. It is undeniable that differences in the setting, the scene, and in the relationship of the participants affect the way in which we speak. Some situations and occasions require a relatively formal manner, while in others casualness is the norm. Employing an inappropriate style can adversely affect the proceedings. There is no neutral style that is suitable for all forms of interaction. Speakers, therefore, must control a range of styles and know which to employ on a given occasion. This is something that is learned as part of the whole process of socialization, and children and adolescents often reveal that they have not fully absorbed the adult social norms (as do some adults too, alas).

Whole books have been written about style, but it remains an elusive concept. Someone once illustrated stylistic differences by rewriting some common proverbs in a more formal style.

It is fruitless to become lachrymose because of scattered lacteal fluid.

A rotating lithoidal fragment never accrues lichen.

Precipitancy creates prodigality.

Pulchritude does not extend below the surface of the derma.

These examples simply illustrate the richness of English vocabulary, but the question of style has been a major problem for all
attempts to study language systematically. It was a particular
problem for those who deal with language as a formal system (see
Chapter 3) when they attempted to characterize meanings on the
basis of combinations of words. One kind of difficulty arises in
dealing with examples that have a similar functional intent but a
very different form and affect, as in the difference between saying
*Would you please keep quiet* and *Shut up!*

Stylistic differences have also caused problems for those who
study social variation in language (see Chapter 5). Studies have
shown social class and gender differences in speech samples, but
these results may be misleading if the examples are recorded in
situations that have different effects on the style recorded. For
examples to be comparable they must be in similar styles, and that
requires controlling for the kinds of factors enumerated in Hymes'
model.

## Instrumentalities

I stands for Instrumentalities, by which Hymes meant the form
of language used, including the distinction between spoken and
written language. As has been pointed out earlier (in Chapter 3)
there are many differences between written and spoken forms of
language and these will be examined further in Chapter 7.

## Norms

N refers to norms of interaction, not only how people behave but
also how they evaluate other people's behavior. There are many
aspects of interaction that we consider "normal" and expect them
to be universal, but then we find that people in other communities
behave differently. This can be seen, for example, in such practices
as greeting someone by kissing on both cheeks, or members of a
family shaking hands at breakfast, or how you hold your knife and
fork. The use of the gestures and facial expressions that accompany
speech also varies according to community standards, not to mention the distance between two people standing having a conversation. There are differences in the speed, loudness, and amount of
speech taken as "normal" in different communities.

## Genre

G, the final letter in the mnemonic, stands for genre. This is a term taken over from literary criticism to distinguish different forms of writing, for example, epic poem, novel, and essay. Genre has been used in linguistics to distinguish between such activities as having a conversation, telling a story, giving a lecture, conducting an interview, and performing a ritual act.

As pointed out in Chapter 1, we use language for many purposes, such as requesting, directing, threatening, promising, informing, inquiring, congratulating, advising, thanking, apologizing, and welcoming. There are "rules" for each of these activities, so that if we violate these rules our behavior will be judged deviant. For example, if someone pays you a compliment, there is an obligation to respond in some way, either to accept it graciously or to demur gently. Compliments come into the category of adjacency pairs in which a failure to respond will be noticed as a violation of expected behavior. On the other hand, insults do not come into this category and it is perfectly acceptable to ignore them. Women are more likely to receive compliments and also to pay them, mainly to other women. Men are more likely to pay compliments to women than to other men. Compliments to women are most often about appearance, whereas compliments to men are more often about ability or possessions. There is some evidence that men find compliments threatening while women find them reassuring.

## Narratives

One exception to the normal rules of turn-taking in a conversation is when someone decides to tell a story. The normal "rules" of turn-taking are suspended when someone is telling a story. In much conversational exchange it is permitted to break in and make a contribution, either to amplify a point that the speaker has made or to disagree with something that has been said. However, it is not normal to interrupt someone in the middle of telling a story. Partly for this reason people often begin with a statement such as *A funny thing happened to me last night* or a question *Can you guess who I saw yesterday in the street?* Such remarks signal that the speaker has a story to tell and the response often counts as permission to tell the whole story. The teller then has the responsibility to make sure that the listeners know where and when the event happened and who the participants were, before going to tell what happened and what the outcome was. The narrator often indicates that the end of the story has been reached by saying something, such as *so that was the last I saw of him*. This signals to the listeners that it is now permissible to participate again in the conversational exchange. It also allows the listeners to show that they have understood the point of the story: *That's amazing!* or *You must be very relieved*. While the story is being told, the listeners are generally restricted to minimal responses or requests for clarification. The "rules" of story-telling are not as rigid as some of the others for ordinary conversation but they are regularly followed. In some cases, however, the narration is shared by more than one speaker, but the same general pattern is followed.

A common feature of storytelling is the creation of suspense. A woman in Dundee told me how she had gone down to the railway station to meet the Dutch sailor who had been her boyfriend years earlier during the war.

> and there I went down
> and no he wasnae on that train
> and went down on the next London train
> no he wasnae on that one
> the one about eleven o'clock in the morning
> and in the late morning the train came in
> there was a lot of pushing and shoving
> and people coming off the trains
> and I'm looking up the platform
> couldnae see him
> I was looking for a Dutch uniform
> couldnae see him
> and then the next thing was this navy blue suit spoke to me you know
> he says "Is that you Bella?"

Notice that Bella tells me four times things that did not happen. It may seem strange that someone should want to tell you what did *not* happen, but the succession of negatives creates the suspense that is resolved when "this navy blue suit" spoke to her.

A good storyteller does not simply report what happened in the most economical way. Instead, details are included that help to create the atmosphere and also to provide some justification for taking the floor to tell the story. If you are telling a story about a dangerous incident in which you were involved, you have to convince the hearers that there was real danger. One way is through the use of quoted dialogue. If in the course of telling the story you say *I almost died*, the hearer may wonder whether you were exaggerating, but if you report someone else as saying *Another inch and you'd have been dead*, that is likely to be much more convincing. It also allows the speaker to get recognition for positive qualities without having to praise oneself, as when one of the Glasgow women reported that someone had said to her *you're the kind of person that would be a good teacher*. Quoted dialogue also makes the story more vivid and allows the listeners to draw their own conclusions about the situation.

## Quoted dialogue

Recently, there has been considerable interest in the use of nontraditional ways of introducing dialogue into stories. The examples below illustrate the range of so-called quotatives (italicized) that have been recorded in recent studies:

> a. I *said* "I think she's away to meet you."
> b. and she *went* "Oh all right."
> c. and I*'m like* "No that's sick."
> d. he*'s all* "You're crazy."

The use of *go* as in (b) was first recorded in 1980 in the United States and later spread to Canada and the United Kingdom. By 1990 forms of *be like*, as in (c) were common among adolescents and university students, again first in the United States but diffusing to other countries. By 2000 there was a wave of popularity for *be all* as in (d) among the same age groups in the United States, but it seems to be receding already and has not spread to other countries. The rapid diffusion of these forms, most of which are believed to have started in California, shows how language change can spread through an age group without affecting the remainder of the population.

Examination of oral narratives produced by people in the course of conversation has shown the great skill with which they are often constructed. What seems on the surface to be a simple story often turns out to have a complex structure that creates its effects in subtle ways. Many details that are not essential to the main plot are often included and add liveliness to the narrative. There is often use of repetition and parallel constructions and other rhetorical devices that are much admired in poetry, though these features were not recognized in everyday storytelling until linguists began recording and analyzing oral narratives.

This chapter shows that the traditional areas of syntax, semantics, and phonetics described in the previous chapters cover only a limited range of the competence that human beings have mastered in order to use language. These skills are not the kind that are taught or evaluated in educational systems. They are learned in the process of interacting with others and they are probably a clearer reflection of an innate ability than any claim about Universal Grammar. The next chapter will examine a different kind of variety in language.

## SUGGESTIONS FOR FURTHER READING

The field of Conversation Analysis was developed by Harvey Sacks, who was killed in a car accident before he was able to present his ideas in a comprehensive form. His *Lectures on Conversation* have been edited by Gail Jefferson and give a good indication of how his ideas emerged. He recorded his class sessions and had them transcribed to be used for discussion at a later date. He circulated copies in dittoed form (this was before photocopying) and I can remember how excited I was to get a new set of lectures. Some of the enthusiasm that Sacks' work provoked can be found in the volume edited by Gene Lerner, entitled *Conversation Analysis: Studies from the First Generation*. R.E. Nofsinger *Everyday Conversation* is an admirably clear introduction to the methods of Conversation Analysis. A more complete account can be found in Emanuel Schegloff's *Sequence Organization in Interaction*. Michael Moerman's *Talking Culture* extends Conversational Analysis beyond the English-speaking world and examines conversational exchanges in Thailand. Robert Hopper's *Telephone Conversation* is a good account of this kind of interaction. Alternative approaches to conversation are presented in Per Linell's *Approaching Dialogue* and *Analyzing Casual Conversation* by Suzanne Eggins and Diana Slade. The uses of silence are explored by Adam Jaworski in *The Power of Silence*.

The use of questions in a variety of situations, including doctor-patient interviews and police interrogations, is examined in a very readable collection of articles *"Why Do You Ask?" The Function of Questions in Institutional Discourse*, edited by Alice Freed and Susan Ehrlich. Cultural differences in conversation are analyzed by Shoshana Blum-Kulka in *Dinner Talk* and by Deborah Tannen in *Conversational Style*.

Dell Hymes' *Foundations in Sociolinguistics* is the source of the SPEAKING mnemonic and other material on language use. Later developments in his approach can be seen in *Now I Know Only So Far: Essays in Ethnopoetics*. The question of style is examined in the articles in *Style and Sociolinguistic Variation*, edited by Penelope Eckert and John Rickford. A different approach to style can be found in Barbara Johnstone's *The Linguistic Individual* that examines the speech styles of several individuals. The use of discourse markers was first fully explored by Deborah Schiffrin in her *Discourse Markers*. The articles in *Small Talk*, edited by Justine Coupland, examine the use of language in a variety of everyday situations.

The examination of oral narratives has been greatly influenced by William Labov's model, which can be found in his *Language in the Inner City*. Barbara Johnstone's *Stories, Community and Place* contains many interesting observations on storytelling. Bella's story about meeting the Dutch sailor is examined more fully in my own *Extremely Common Eloquence* along with a number of other very effective narratives told by a range of Scottish speakers.

# 5

# Language as Identity

The variety of language that surrounds us is quite remarkable. From the moment we emerge into William James's world of "booming, buzzing confusion," our brains are actively trying to interpret the range of sensory information that bombards us. We have to learn to make discriminations in all the senses, adjusting to differences between hot and cold, between dark and light, and so on. Perhaps the most important sense for human beings is hearing, because language is so important for our daily lives. In developing the ability to communicate their needs and desires, young children are also discovering that there are other features of language that help to identify the speaker. For example, at a very early age, infants will distinguish their mother's voice from that of strangers. At a later age it is common to recognize a speaker on the telephone, with no prior notice of who is making the call. In terms of communicative efficiency, with a single emphasis on the meaning of the utterance, such associated signals of identity are often irrelevant. In terms of social cohesion, such features are of immense importance. The preceding chapters focused on different ways of looking at language essentially as a system for communicating meaning, as generally understood. The present chapter examines a different aspect of meaning in a basic function of language that is important to social organization in every society, namely how we present ourselves to others and how we are perceived by them.

Although no two individuals are identical, we share some characteristics with other family members, with people of our own age and sex, with members of our surrounding community, and so on. The way we dress, the food we eat, the ways in which we amuse ourselves are likely to be fairly consistent with how others in our community behave. In the same way, how we speak is affected by our place in society and this usually makes it possible for a stranger to draw some inferences about our social background simply from hearing us speak. It also often makes it easy for members of a community to identify an outsider. The study of linguistic differences related to social factors is the province of sociolinguistics, which has been a separate division of linguistics for about fifty years, and dialectology, which has a much longer history.

## Dialectology

As we have seen in previous chapters, linguists have not found it easy to deal with the fact that all the speakers of a language do not speak in exactly the same way. Consequently, linguists have resorted to a variety of idealizations, from Chomsky's "ideal speaker-listener" (Chapter 3) to Daniel Jones's definition of a language as "the speech of one individual pronouncing in a definite and consistent style" (Chapter 2). Some of the reasons for this approach were for principles of linguistic theory, others were for practical reasons. Prior to the development of relatively simple (and portable) instruments for recording sound, it was necessary for the investigator to transcribe what the speaker said into some form of notation. To meet the needs of scholars studying different languages (or different dialects of the same language), a form of transcription was developed to represent all the sounds found in human language which could be consistently interpreted. This system is known as the **International Phonetic Alphabet** (IPA) and it is the standard for representing the sounds of speech in any language. (The IPA charts for consonants and vowels were given in Chapter 2.)

Nineteenth century linguists in Europe were very conscious that there were many differences in the ways in which people in different parts of a country spoke. They created the field of dialect geography to chart these differences and developed techniques to collect information. Fieldworkers were trained to elicit forms from a sample of speakers and transcribe the results in phonetic notation. Because of a belief that the dialects were an older form of the language, the speakers were chosen to reflect this usage. In practice, this meant that most of those interviewed were non-mobile, older, rural males (NORMS for short). Surveys for *The Linguistic Atlas of the United States and Canada* started in the 1930s, and *The Survey of English Dialects* was carried out in the 1950s. The collection of this information was very time-consuming, as the interviews could last anything up to ten hours for the American survey and up to twenty-four hours for the English one (obviously not in a single session). The main emphases were on pronunciation and vocabulary. Moreover, recording speech by manual transcription is a tedious procedure, which often requires repetitions of single words (or expressions) until the investigator is satisfied that the representation will give an accurate account of the form. Unfortunately, the forms transcribed give only a partial indication of the way in which the interviewees speak, because people do not communicate by uttering words in isolation as clearly as possible.

The Linguistic Atlas of Scotland (LAS) avoided the problems of interviewing by sending out questionnaires by mail and documented a considerable amount of valuable information about regional differences in language. LAS uncovered a wide variety of terms for items that were familiar to those living in rural areas. For example, LAS collected more than fifty different terms for the plant foxglove, of which a sample is given in Table 5.1.

Table 5.1   Some names for foxglove
in The Linguistic Atlas of Scotland

| **Foxglove** (*digitalis*) |
| --- |
| lady's finger |
| witch's thimble |
| fairy finger |
| fairy thimble |
| dead man's finger |
| dead man's bell |
| bloody man's finger |
| witch's pap |
| bloody finger |
| trowie glove |

Methods of collecting information about differences in language changed with the development of the portable tape recorder. This invention made it possible to record speakers in relatively informal and relaxed conditions and to study connected speech rather than isolated words. Thus it was possible to study both variation within the community and also variation in the way an individual speaker uses language on different occasions. This development required a completely new methodology for collecting samples of speech.

## Sociolinguistics

In 1963, William Labov published in the journal *Word* an article entitled "The social motivation of a sound change." This article had an impact on the study of language variation similar to the effect of Chomsky's *Syntactic Structures* on the study of syntax. Labov showed that on the island of Martha's Vineyard, off the Massachusetts coast, there was a change taking place in the way in which the inhabitants pronounced the diphthongs /ay/ in words such as *tide* and /aw/ in words such as *house*. Some speakers were beginning the articulation of the diphthong with the tongue higher in the mouth, a process known as centralization. (In the articulation of these diphthongs the tongue moves from a low central position to a higher position, close to a high front vowel in the case of /ay/ and to a high back rounded vowel in the case of /aw/.) Labov had found differences in the extent to which different categories of the speakers he interviewed participated in the change. Factors such as the age of the speaker, where he or she lived, and which ethnic group they belonged to affected their participation in the change. Fishermen showed the most centralization and farmers the least, but attitude toward life on the island turned out to be the factor that had the strongest influence. Those who felt positive about island life had adopted the new pronunciation, while those who preferred life on the mainland tended to avoid it.

Table 5.2   Centralization and attitudes about life on Martha's Vineyard

|                   | ay     | aw     |
|-------------------|--------|--------|
| Positive attitude | high   | high   |
| Neutral attitude  | lower  | lower  |
| Negative attitude | lowest | lowest |

The centralized diphthongs resembled the kind of speech that the original settlers probably used, so the use of such forms could be understood as a return to a traditional way of speaking. The Martha's Vineyard study was a clear demonstration of the interaction of many factors that contribute to language variation and change.

Labov was able to show this because of the way in which he coded his results. He developed a scale with four intervals based on tongue height and assigned a value to each token of all the words on the tape that included the diphthongs /ay/ and /aw/. He then summed up the values for each speaker and obtained an average score for each diphthong. He could then calculate an average score for a social category, for example, those aged 61–75, or those who lived in the community of Chilmark, or those who were of Portuguese ancestry. These group scores could then be compared with another example from the same category, for example, those aged 31–45 or those who lived in Edgartown. This quantitative approach allowed comparison on a range of social factors and provided a model for future investigations of linguistic variation.

## The study of urban varieties

The development of this new methodology transformed the study of language variation by making it possible to chart the hetero-geneity of urban speech. Prior to Labov's pioneering work, those interested in language variation had tended to focus on regional differences, using traditional methods of eliciting different words and expressions from older rural speakers. Labov followed up his own example by conducting a large-scale investigation in New York City. Labov's account of this study, *The Social Stratification of English in New York City*, soon became the model for other investigations of urban speech in Detroit, Anniston (Alabama), Reading (England), Montreal (Canada), Glasgow (Scotland), Sydney (Australia), and Bahia Blanca (Argentina). These studies revealed the systematic nature of linguistic differences related to social stratification and also ethnicity. In recent years, however, there have been fewer community studies of this kind, since most investigators have focused their attention on sub-groups or single features.

## Regional differences

The sociolinguistic focus on urban speech did not interrupt the investigation of regional differences. In 1965, work on the *Dictionary of American Regional English* (DARE) was begun and within five years field workers had collected information from a thousand communities across the nation. The first four volumes of the dictionary have already appeared and the fifth will be published soon. DARE has assembled a vast collection of words that are used regionally rather than nationally (Table 5.3).

Table 5.3   Some regional expressions from the Dictionary of American Regional English

**antigodlin** adj. lopsided, askew, out of line

**goozle** n. the throat, gullet, windpipe, or Adam's apple

**goozlum** n. a viscous food such as a sauce or gravy

**lagniappe** n. a small gratuity or bonus

**mulligrubs** n.pl. a condition of despondency or ill-temper

**nebby** adj. nosy, inquisitive

**pipjenny** n. a pimple

**rantum scoot** n. an outing with no definite destination

The materials collected in several American dialect atlas projects have now been housed at the University of Georgia in the Linguistic Atlas Projects and scholars are continuing to analyze this material. Lee Pederson's monumental *Linguistic Atlas of the Gulf States* was the first American survey to employ a sampling method that balances regional and social characteristics. Traditional linguistic atlas projects have taken a long time to collect the information but the improvement in the quality of telephone signals allowed Labov and his associates to carry out a national survey in a very short period of time. They interviewed over 700 speakers from a wide range of locations and have been able to chart certain changes in progress. One of the most widespread is the loss of the contrast between the vowels in words such as *cot* and *caught*, or the names *Don* and *Dawn*. This change has spread to West in recent years and in many areas it is mainly older speakers who will still make any distinction.

Another development in the study of regional variation is what is known as Folk Dialectology. This approach investigates, by a variety of methods, the attitudes of speakers to other regional forms of speech. Studies have shown that many people have distinct opinions about how people in other parts of the country speak. For example, inhabitants of Michigan believe that their own form of speech is more "correct" than that of any other region and they have a particularly low opinion of the speech of those who live in New York City and the South (particularly Alabama). They also find their own speech and that of their neighboring states "pleasant," in contrast again to that of New York City and also (somewhat surprisingly) the South. The inhabitants of Indiana, on the other hand, agree that Southern speech is less "correct" but they find it "pleasant." Folk dialectology is still in a developmental stage but it promises to provide some new insights into how speakers view their own speech and that of others.

## Investigating language variation

In the past forty years, many other aspects of language variation have been systematically investigated by sociolinguists. Some investigators have used ethnographic methods, which involve extended observation of the use of language in a community, but most sociolinguists have followed Labov's example of basing their analysis on recorded samples of speech from a range of speakers. These recordings are then analyzed to identify the features (if any) that distinguish people in one social category from those in another. This method is sometimes referred to as Labovian sociolinguistics, and sometimes as quantitative sociolinguistics or variationist sociolinguistics.

## Sociolinguistic methodology

The portable tape recorder, however, did not in itself solve the problems of describing this variation, because the circumstances in which the recording is made will affect the kind of speech recorded. As pointed out in Chapter 4, all speakers vary their form of speech according to the person they are addressing, the situation, the topic, and so on. In fact, far from solving all the problems of studying language variation, the tape recorder has introduced a new set of problems. In order to investigate variation within a community, sociolinguists usually identify a target sample of speakers to be recorded. Ideally, one would like to make sure that all sectors of the community are included, but any project is limited in time and money, so compromises are usually necessary.

Although a variety of methods have been adopted, the common principle is that the sample should be chosen by some objective process. In other words, the investigator should not chose speakers specifically to support a particular hypothesis. On the other hand, a totally random sample (unless it were very large) might not provide adequate representation of certain social categories. Depending upon the community, most sociolinguists will want to have a sample that includes roughly equal numbers of both sexes, various age groups, and covers the range of socio-economic categories. In some communities, religion or ethnicity may also be significant factors affecting language variation, and it will be necessary to consider these factors when selecting the sample. Then there is the problem of identifying members of the population who fit into each category. Age and gender are relatively straightforward but social class is trickier. The simplest classifier for this has turned out to be occupation, though some studies have employed complex socio-economic indices.

Labov had the advantage of being able to make use of a systematic sociological survey of the Lower East Side in New York City that interviewed almost a thousand respondents. From this sample Labov was able to interview a stratified sample of 122 speakers from a range of different ethnic backgrounds. The sample was also stratified by social class and gender, though the highest social class was underrepresented and women outnumbered men by two to one.

The size of the sample in a sociolinguistic survey is also problematic. It might appear that the larger it is, the better, but practical considerations place a limit on what is feasible. In the first place, it takes time and effort to record an adequate number of speakers. Second, the processing of analyzing the recordings is extremely time-consuming. Consequently, it is rare to find a sociolinguistic study with more than a hundred speakers and there may be as few as twelve. However, it has been shown that even a small sample can provide a revealing account of the speech variation in a community, because many features will vary in a systematic fashion throughout the community.

In my own investigation in Glasgow, the sample of 48 contained equal numbers of 10-year-olds, 15-year-olds, and adults in four social class categories, with equal numbers of males and females in each category, with Protestants outnumbering Catholics two to one. This provided information on social class, age, and gender differences in the use of several variables, though the numbers in each category were small.

Deciding on the size and nature of the sample is only one of the challenges facing the investigator. There is the question of how and where to make the recordings. The most common technique is to interview each speaker separately. This has the advantage that the voices of the interviewer and the interviewee can be clearly distinguished and the quality of the recorded sound can be quite high. This depends also on where the interview is held. Interviewing people at work may be impractical because of the ambient noise. Many interviews, therefore, are held at the speaker's home (though this is not always a noise-free atmosphere either). In order for the samples to be comparable, it is best for the speakers to be recorded in similar circumstances. The interviewing of children, however, is often done at school.

More important than the place of the recording is the relationship between the interviewer and the interviewee. The interviewer has the responsibility of creating a suitable atmosphere for the interview. Ideally, the person being interviewed should feel comfortable in the situation and be able to talk in a relaxed manner. Differences of age, status or ethnicity may cause awkwardness, and thus affect the quality of speech recorded. In an interview, it also makes a difference whether the interviewer is a man or a woman. Same-sex conversations have been shown to be different from cross-sex ones. There was some criticism of early sociolinguistic accounts of gender differences because the interviewers had all been male, though many of those interviewed were female, but there is no easy answer to this problem. Arranging to have males only interviewed by males and females by females complicates the research design and even then does not guarantee equivalent results. Social class and ethnic differences are even more complex, not to mention the situation of adults interviewing children. On the other hand, it has been shown that in many cases strangers talking to each other tend to accommodate to the other person's style of speech (Chapter 4). As a result, the speech recorded in the interview may not be a good example of the speaker's normal speech.

Some investigators have tried to avoid this problem by arranging sessions with a group of speakers, but there are many problems with this approach. Unless each speaker is recorded on a separate track, it may be difficult to distinguish the voices. Moreover, people who do not know each other may not feel relaxed in a group situation. A method that has recently been employed is to have two people who know each other talk together without the investigator present. This method proved particularly effective in getting good samples of adolescent speech in Glasgow (see below).

This examination of the practical problems involved in recording samples of speech is important because the data are at the center of sociolinguistic research. It is not enough to make a claim about the social distribution of a certain feature in a given community. It is necessary to state explicitly how the data on which this claim is made were collected. The empirical basis of sociolinguistic research depends upon a rigorous methodology that will allow confirmation of the results through a replication of the study. In strong contrast to the introspective and casual methods of the theoretical linguists discussed in Chapter 3, the validity and reliability of sociolinguistic research depends upon careful attention to the ways in which the data are collected. Despite the many problems involved in collecting appropriate samples of speech, however, sociolinguists have succeeded in identifying many features of speech that vary systematically with social factors.

**Social differences**

The differences in the way people speak provide certain kinds of information about the speakers and this information forms part of their identity. However, not all features of speech are appropriate for sociolinguistic investigation. As Labov put it in introducing his pioneering study of Lower East Side, New York, here are many kinds of variation that are not appropriate for linguistic analysis, including lisp, stammer, and other physiological idiosyncrasies. Similarly, variations in tempo, pitch, volume, and nasality are not usually typical of group characteristics. Consequently, sociolinguists have paid little attention to paralinguistic features of this kind, although some of them may in fact have social significance.

The challenge for those who wish to describe social variation in language is thus how to do so in a systematic way that will allow comparison between speakers and between groups of speakers. Since we all vary our speech according to the particular situation we are in, it is not enough simply to collect a set of individual examples of speech forms, since we may use one in one context and another in a different context. In order to identify typical characteristics of someone's speech we need to collect samples systematically. One approach to this problem has been to look at frequencies: how often a speaker uses a particular form. It is not the overall frequency of any form that is important but its frequency of occurrence in a particular context. Those items that vary in ways that are of interest to sociolinguists are called **linguistic variables** and each variable will have two or more **variants**. As pointed out above, the breakthrough in sociolinguistics came with Labov's demonstration of a way to quantify the differences in the use of variants so as to make possible comparison between speakers.

For variables with only two variants, a simple percentage will be adequate. For example, in the investigation I carried out in Glasgow, I identified two variants for the sound [t] in words such as *butter* and *hit*. One of the variants is a normal [t], the other a glottal stop [ʔ], such as the sound often heard for [t] in words such as *mountain*. As there were only two variants, I could record the results as the percentage of glottal stops in words where the two possibilities existed. (There are some contexts in which glottal stops are not possible, for example, at the beginning of words.) I searched the recordings for examples of words where glottal stops could occur and noted whether a glottal stop had been produced or not. In this way I was able to create a score for glottal stops for every speaker I had recorded and to compare their usage. The frequency of a glottal stop before a following vowel or a pause ranged from 0% to 100% among the adults. Then I calculated the average use of glottal stops for one of the categories of speakers that I had chosen to study. For example, the working-class 15-year-old boys used glottal stops 90% of the time before a vowel, compared

108    *Seven Ways of Looking at Language*

with middle-class boys of the same age (49%), working-class women (77%), or middle-class adults (18%). As glottal stops were evaluated unfavorably, it is not surprising that the frequency of glottal stops was higher in the recordings of the lower-class speakers. There were also gender differences, in that the middle-class women used fewer glottal stops than the middle-class men. Such results would not surprise anyone who was familiar with a range of Glasgow speakers, but I was able to show quite clearly how the differences in pronunciation correlated closely with membership in social class categories. Figure 5.1 shows the increasing use of glottal stops from the highest social class to the lowest and also the differences between men and woman, particularly in the lower-middle class.

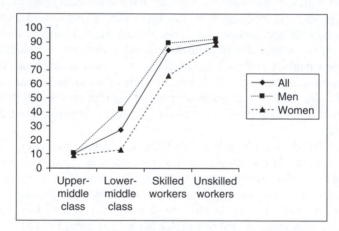

Figure 5.1    Frequency of glottal stops in Glasgow

Linguistic variables that have more than two variants require more complicated measures. Most difficult of all are vowels because they vary continuously along at least one dimension. As pointed out above, this problem was solved by William Labov in his studies on Martha's Vineyard and in New York City. Labov developed a scale for each variant, with a numerical value based on, for example, tongue height, and then averaged the values for that vowel for a particular speaker. This gave an index for that variable for each speaker. These methods of quantifying variation have been widely employed and have proved very successful in charting the range and importance of language variation in numerous communities. Later methods, also pioneered by Labov, employ acoustic analysis to chart the differences in vowel quality.

The social factors related to linguistic differences that have received the most attention are Age, Gender, Social Class, and Ethnicity. In a wide range of studies, it has been shown that, apart from individual differences, the use of linguistic variables may reflect membership in a social group that is defined by one of these categories. It is hardly surprising that this should be so. At a national level we recognize individuals as belonging to our community by the language they speak, and we identify outsiders by the fact that they speak differently. Sometimes these forms become the subject of overt comment, but such stereotypes are usually the residue of older ways of speaking that have become largely obsolete by the time they are widely recognized. The kinds of features that sociolinguists investigate are more subtle differences, mostly in pronunciation, but it is also possible to investigate differences in the use of words. In two separate studies in Scotland I found that middle-class speakers use the words *very* and *quite* much more frequently than working-class speakers did (Figure 5.2).

The social class difference in the use of *very* in the Glasgow sample is remarkable and is highly significant. Half of the working-class Glasgow adults do not use *very* even once. There is also a

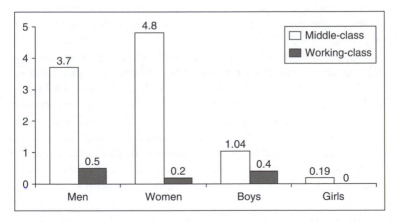

Figure 5.2　Social class differences in the use of *very* in Glasgow (frequency per 1,000 words)

significant age difference. The adolescents use *very* significantly less than the adults (both groups of adolescents barely use *very*). There is no significant gender difference.

## Regional differences

Language serves a dual function. It has a unifying function, creating a community through a shared form of speech, but it also has a separatist function, distinguishing us from others who speak differently. In fact, one of the defining characteristics of a nation is often language, and new nations emerging from domination by an imperial power usually adopt a national language as a sign of independence. Within a country there are often similar distinctions, though the boundaries are usually less clear. This is partly because local variations in language (dialect differences) are usually not recorded in a consistent written form (see Chapter 7). There are, however, forms of speech that are identified with a particular region of a country. In the United States, for example, most people can recognize a Southern accent and many New Yorkers are easily identifiable by their speech. In Britain, there are even more marked differences between the inhabitants of southern England and those of Scotland and Wales. Regional differences are often referred to as dialects, but this is a notoriously difficult term to define or interpret. Such differences have been studied for more than a hundred years by dialect geographers and they have often presented their results in the form of maps showing the distribution of variant forms (Figure 5.3).

This map shows one of the major differences between northern and southern varieties of English. The line runs roughly from the river Humber in the east to the river Ribble in the west and marks the boundary of several important differences in pronunciation. South of this line, in Old English times, the low back unrounded vowel in words such as *hām* and *bān* became a rounded vowel as in the modern descendants *home* and *bone*. In Scotland, where this change did not take place you can still encounter speakers who say *hame* and *bane*. In fact, the rhyme I learned as a child was:

Sticks and stanes
May break my banes
But names'll never hurt me

Figure 5.3    Map of a major dialect boundary in England

Regional differences largely exist for historical reasons. In both Britain and the United States, much of the variation in dialect follows from differences in the speech of early settlers (see Chapter 6). But the persistence of significant differences usually has a social or a political basis. It is hardly surprising that there are marked differences in speech on either side of the "border" between England and Scotland, although there are few other features to distinguish people on one side from those on the other. For example, to close friends, I often end a letter with the expression *Yours aye*, that is equivalent to "Yours always." This use of *aye* for "always" is restricted to speakers north of the border between England and Scotland as was established by the responses recorded in *The Linguistic Atlas of Scotland*.

Similarly, in the United States, the Mason-Dixon Line is often cited as the boundary between northern and southern speech, although the differences are relatively minor. Most Americans when asked to give an indication of regional differences in speech mention "the South" as an identifiable region. At a different level, the inhabitants of a city (e.g., Glasgow in Scotland, Liverpool in England, Pittsburgh in the United States) may have certain features that make their speech distinctive in ways that are recognizable to the inhabitants themselves as well as to outsiders. Labor's telephone survey of 762 speakers in urban areas throughout the United States shows how widespread variation is. It also shows how some changes are progressing in different parts of the country (see Chapter 6).

Even recent everyday items can show regional differences. In many delicatessens in the United States it is possible to purchase a sandwich that consists of a long roll filled with cold meat, cheese, lettuce, and condiments. This sandwich, generally known as a *submarine*, probably because of it shape, goes by a variety of names in different parts of the country (Table 5.4).

Table 5.4    Local terms for a Submarine sandwich

| Submarine |
| --- |
| *hero* New York City |
| *hoagie* Philadelphia |
| *wedge* Westchester Co., New York |
| *po' boy* New Orleans |
| *torpedo* Troy, Albany |
| *grinder* New England |
| *zep* Norristown, Pennsylvania |

## Age differences

Obviously, in every society there is a wide range of age among the speakers and this may affect the way in which they speak. The clearest cases are those of very young children, whose language differs substantially from that of the adults around them, but even when children have reached the age of, say, ten, when they are able to communicate easily with adults, there will be differences that may not be apparent in casual interactions. Much of education consists in learning language, particularly vocabulary. At the other end of the spectrum, the very old may use words and expressions that are not current among the younger generations. They may also deplore the kind of language used by younger people. Such differences between the generations are obvious to anyone but there are sometimes more subtle differences that are revealed under systematic investigation.

There are also obvious differences in pronunciation. We can easily distinguish a child's voice from that of an adult, since the size of the vocal tract affects the pitch of the voice. One of the important sex differences is that in boys at puberty the larynx increases in size, causing a lengthening of the vocal cords, which in turn lowers the pitch of the voice. Such disruption to articulation is sometimes referred to as the boy's voice "breaking." This change does not occur in girls. Prior to puberty the pitch of boys' and girls' voices is very similar but after puberty the adult difference in pitch between male and female voices becomes established.

Physiological changes such as these are not of great interest to sociolinguists because they occur in the population at large. There are no social factors that affect the process. In the preschool period, children will generally speak a similar form of language to their parents. This may change when they go to school where they are exposed to the language of their peers, which may differ noticeably from that of the home.

For example, in Glasgow I found that the upper-middle-class 10-year-olds were more similar to their working-class peers in their use of glottal stops than their parents were to working-class adults. An even greater difference was shown by the lower-middle-class 10-year-olds and 15-year-olds, as can be seen in Figure 5.4. One possible explanation is that the middle-class children had been influenced by their working-class peers.

Such differences are even more likely to occur when a linguistic change is in progress (see Chapter 6). For example, Labov found that in New York City in the 1960s a change was taking place that affected the sound represented by the letter "r" in words such as *car* and *card*. Varieties of English differ in the way in which words of this type are pronounced. In so-called **rhotic varieties**, the "r" is pronounced by a bunching of the tongue of the tongue in the center of the mouth, which produces an /r/ sound. In non-rhotic varieties, there is no such articulation or sound and the "r" is signaled only by a slight lengthening of the vowel. Most varieties of American English are rhotic, as are Scottish and Northern English. Southern

British English, Bostonian, and some varieties of American southern speech are non-rhotic.

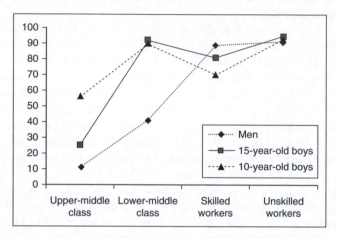

Figure 5.4    Age differences in the use of glottal stops in Glasgow

Prior to World War II, New York City was **non-rhotic,** but after the war a change occurred. This did not happen suddenly but gradually spread, as changes generally do. Labov was able to show that the change was occurring fastest in the highest socio-economic group and that this was particularly true of the younger speakers. He also found that older middle-class speakers were more likely to participate in the change than younger speakers from the same socio-economic group.

Age differences in language use have been reported in a number of sociolinguistic studies, but age is not as simple a category as it might seem. It is usually easy to determine a speaker's age, at least approximately, but it is much harder to assign individuals to groups according to age. It is simple to distinguish preschool children from those of elementary school age, but then what? Are those in Junior High School a separate category from High School students? After High School there is a category of young adults, but at what age do you cease to be a young adult and become simply an adult? Then when do middle age and old age begin? Sociolinguists have tended to divide up the age continuum in somewhat arbitrary ways and often settle for relatively simple categories.

In a set of Glasgow conversations that I analyzed, there were two distinct age categories: adolescents, aged 13–14, and adults in their 40s, recorded in same-sex pairs without the investigator present. The conversations show a clear distinction between adolescents and adults, but offer no information about the use of language by speakers outside of these two age groups. Consequently, it is impossible to say from this study at what age (if ever) the adolescents would become more similar in language usage to the adults, but there were a number of clear differences. Under the same recording situation, the adults as a group produced many more words than the adolescents, though in both groups some speakers were more talkative than others, and there is overlap between the two age groups.

The adolescents asked more questions of each other and more often told their partners to do something using an imperative. In comparison with the adults, the adolescents seldom used the adverbs *very* (see chart above) and *quite*, though the use of the word *just* was similar between the two age groups. The adults were more likely to use expressions with the articles *the* and *a/an*, and the adolescents used more pronouns. The adults employed the discourse markers *well*, *you know*, and *I mean* quite frequently while the adolescents seldom used them. On the other hand, the adolescents used the word *like* in manners similar to their counterparts in the United States in examples such as: *I like get three pounds a week* and *I think someone like reported him*. The adolescents also used *like* as a way of introducing dialogue in a narrative: *and I'm like "No that's sick"* and *I'm like "Woops."*

One feature of the Glasgow adolescents' speech was their use of intensifiers (words to emphasize a quality). Some examples are: *I'd look **dead** funny without a fringe wouldn't I?*, *this is **dead** embarrassing*, *this is **pure** embarrassing*, and *I was standing **pure** close to him*. There is also a new form *healthy* that is just appearing, as in *that's a **healthy** phone innit* (meaning that it is a good one).

From Figure 5.5, we can see that *healthy* is used more frequently by the older adolescents and that boys use it more frequently than girls.

## Social class differences

Social class has been shown to be related to variation in many aspects of language. The majority of studies have dealt with

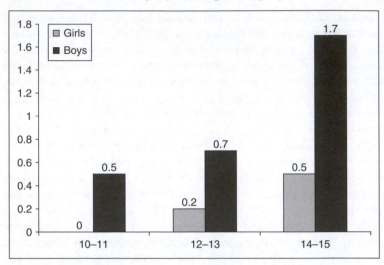

Figure 5.5    Use of healthy by Glasgow adolescents

differences in pronunciation. Differences in vowel quality have been found to correlate with social class differences in a number of studies in New York City, Reading (England), Glasgow (Scotland) and Londonderry (Northern Ireland). Interestingly, even more robust correlations have often been found for consonants in New York City, Detroit, Reading, Glasgow, Cardiff, Newcastle, and Londonderry. This may be because consonantal variables are often stable sociolinguistic features (i.e., not part of any change), though the recent spread of glottal stops in Britain from the southeast is an obvious exception. The use of glottal stops at one time was most frequent only among lower-class speakers in certain urban areas, especially London and Glasgow. In recent years the use of glottal stops has spread upward socially even to upper-middle-class speakers and regionally throughout most of England. What used to be a highly stigmatized form is now much more widely accepted.

There are also social class differences in intonation but these have not been investigated systematically, so it is not clear how significant these differences are. That situation is likely to change with developments in instrumental techniques of measurement, including the digitizing of speech on computers. One investigator has ventured into paralinguistic phenomena and examined social class differences in voice quality in Glasgow. Jane Stuart-Smith found that working-class Glaswegian voice quality had the features of more open jaw position, raised and backed tongue body with possible retracted tongue root, and whispery voice. This helps to account for the distinctive timbre of Glasgow working-class speech. As far as the middle-class Glaswegians are concerned she observes that their voice quality "is best described in terms of the *absence* of W[orking] C[lass] traits." A similar point could be made about most social class differences in pronunciation. The middle-class speakers of the standard variety of the language tend to use fewer of the sounds that identify speakers with a particular location. In this sense, middle-class speech is more neutral, and there is more variety to be found in working-class vernacular speech. The term **vernacular** is regularly used by sociolinguists to refer to the form of speech used by speakers when they are relaxed and not worrying about conforming to some notion of "correctness."

In morphology social class differences have been found in tense marking. In Norwich, England, for example, omission of third person singular −s as in *he go* was found to be characteristic of lower-class speakers but not of middle-class speakers. Social class differences in forms of negation have also been found in widely different communities. A study in Anniston, Alabama showed that there were social class and gender differences in the use of *done* as an auxiliary and double modals (e.g., *she might could be a big help to you*) and the quasi-modal *liketa* (e.g., *she liketa had a heart attack!*).

Other studies have shown social class differences in the use relative pronouns. In Ayr, in Scotland, I found that the middle-class speakers were much more likely to use *wh*-relatives (i.e., *who, which*) than the working-class speakers. In investigations in Ayr and Glasgow I found that working-class speakers used significantly fewer derived adverbs (e.g., *definitely, seriously*) and intensifiers such as *very* than the middle-class speakers. The working-class speakers also used more modal auxiliaries. The middle-class speakers used more passives and more evaluative adjectives, as well as hedges, such as *sort of, kind of,* and *quite*. The working-class speakers also were more likely to use "dislocated syntax," that is an order which brings certain items into prominence. Some examples are given in Table 5.5.

Table 5.5    Examples of dislocated syntax from working-class interviews in Ayr

---

Focusing
*and that was you shut in the house for a week*

Clefting
*it's a queer man and wife that doesnae have an argument*

Right dislocation
*she was a very quiet woman my mother*

Left dislocation
*Mr. Patterson he was a gentleman*

Noun Phrase preposing
*An auld man he was you ken*

---

In both Ayr and Glasgow there were clear social class differences in discourse style, each effective in its own way. The middle-class speakers were more willing to talk about how they think and feel, while the working-class speakers were more reticent about their personal feelings and attitudes. There is no reason to claim that one style of speaking is superior to the other.

In New York, Labov found linguistic differences in the pronunciation of consonants and vowels that correlated with social factors such as ethnicity, religion, and socio-economic status. Equally important was the discovery that New Yorkers were generally aware of the social significance of these differences. This awareness, however, did not lead speakers in the lowest socio-economic groups to avoid forms that they knew to be stigmatized by other members of their community. This finding has been corroborated by studies in Britain, where social class differences are much more salient than in the United States. In general, people speak the way that is typical of their social group. It is one signal of this aspect of their social identity, though it is not the whole story.

**Ethnic differences**

Social class differences have received more attention in Britain than in the United States, probably because social class distinctions are more salient in Britain. In the United States there has been more emphasis on ethnic differences. In the 1960s, with the impact of the Civil Rights movement, attention was focused on the speech of Black Americans. The labels for this variety changed over the years from Non-Standard Negro Speech, to Black English, to African American English, and now the most commonly used term is **African American Vernacular English (AAVE)**. It also has connotations of lower social status because people of higher status are assumed to use "standard" forms even when speaking casually.

The early work on AAVE was to some extent motivated by a desire to show that vernacular forms of speech are as regular and systematic as the standard language. One impressive study, carried out by William Labov, investigated the speech of African American males aged 8–19 who participated in the street culture of New York City. Labov was able to show that grammatical patterns not found in the standard language were used consistently and systematically by these speakers.

---

**Examples of AAVE**

*I was like to have got shot*
*I might can't get no more fines neither*
*ain't nothing happening*
*don't nobody break up a fight.*
*I done told on that*
*she be standing with her hand in her pocket*

---

Labov was able to show that these forms were not "mistakes" but examples of constructions that are grammatical for the speakers. Other features of AAVE include the absence of possessive marking (*at my mama house*), absence of third person singular marking (*she have three kids*), omission of the verb *be* (*she in the same grade*), and the use of *it* rather than *there* (*it's some coffee in the kitchen*). Although Labov and other sociolinguists have demonstrated in many academic publications that these constructions are systematic in AAVE, the general public has remained unconvinced. This was obvious in the acrimonious debate that followed the decision of the Oakland school board to recognize "Ebonics" as a distinct language. Ebonics is not a term that most sociolinguists would employ but they were forced to use it in their efforts to contradict the negative attitudes to AAVE that were evident in the media.

Some of the problems sociolinguists have faced in their attempts to convince the public of the value of AAVE stem from the fact that the most vernacular users are adolescents and teenage language use of any variety is often criticized for being sloppy or ungrammatical. Although sociolinguists have succeeded in demonstrating to each other that AAVE has a distinct structure that can be used consistently by its speakers, it is very difficult to persuade many members of the public (including teachers) that these apparently ungrammatical forms are not simply mistakes.

Despite the growing numbers, less attention has been paid to those from Spanish-speaking backgrounds. Once again there have been changes in the terminology, from Mexican American English to Chicano English and Latino English. The characteristics of Latino English are less dramatically different from Anglo-American varieties, with the most obvious being differences in pronunciation. Interestingly, many of the differences are not typical of the forms used by native speakers of Spanish who are learning English, so Latino English is not simply a version of a foreign accent. Moreover, many speakers of Latino English were born in the United States and they do not all come from Mexico. There are Puerto-Rican, Cuban, and Dominican forms of Latino English and they all have distinct characteristics. As with other social categories the distinctive forms of Latino English are a signal of identity.

One characteristic of many Latino speakers is their ability to code-switch between English and Spanish. At one time this code-switching was interpreted as indicating a lack of proficiency in one (or both) of the languages, but studies of bilingual situations in many parts of the world have shown that code-switching is a stylistic device used for a variety of communicative purposes. It does not reflect any deficiency in the language. Here is an example from a 45-year-old Mexican American man who has lived all his life in Los Angeles. He switches back and forth between the languages because he is comfortable in both.

But I am the only one that came out *músico*. My – all my brothers were into sports, basketball, baseball, *y todo*, and I couldn't do that. *No me gustaban.* I could, you know, play *y todo, pero a mi me gustaba más la guitarra.*
(But I am the only one that came out a *musician*. My – all my brothers were into sports, basketball, baseball, *and everything*, and I couldn't do that. *I didn't like them.* I could, you know, play *and everything, but I liked the guitar more.*

Among African American and Latino youths "white" can be used as a derogatory term for those in their community who use "proper English" or standard pronunciations. John Rickford quotes a comment from an African American teenager: "Over at my school...first time they catch you talkin' white, they'll never let it go." Any feature that is assumed to be standard is associated with white speakers. The link between ethnic identity and language is clearly demonstrated.

An example of a new ethnic variety is the emergence of Cajun Vernacular English in Louisiana. The Cajuns are the descendants of French-speaking immigrants who came from Canada in the 18th century and continued to speak French. In recent years French has been losing ground to English but a characteristic variety of Cajun English has developed in which younger speakers are using forms that were once used by older speakers but had been dropping out. Features that had once been stigmatized are being adopted as signals of Cajun identity.

## Gender differences

Early sociolinguistic discussion of gender differences occurred in the context of investigations that focused mainly on social class differences. It appeared in a number of studies that women used more of the standard variants than men while men, particularly lower-class men, seemed more anxious to assert their toughness through the use of nonstandard forms, perhaps as a way of distancing themselves from a feminine world. Later studies have shown that women are often the leaders in linguistic changes (see Chapter 6), thus contradicting the notion that women are generally more conservative in language usage.

Peter Trudgill, in his investigation of variation in Reading, England, found that men were more likely than women to use the alveolar nasal [n] for forms ending in –*ing*, a phenomenon erroneously known as "dropping the *g*" although there is no [g] pronounced in words such as *running* and *shouting*. The difference can be seen in Figure 5.6, based on Peter Trudgill's findings. There are clear social class differences as well as gender ones, with the working-class speakers showing a greater tendency to use [n].

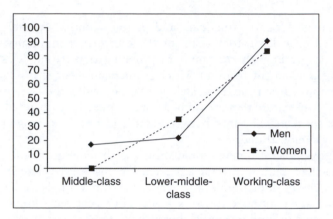

Figure 5.6    Percentage of –in [n] for ing [ŋ] in Reading in 1971

Ethnographic studies of adolescent speech behavior have shown girls making greater use of language differences to establish their identity in school-based groups or street gangs. Membership in these groups is influenced by social class categories but participation in certain group activities has more impact on the girls than on the boys. It has also been argued that women are more cooperative and polite in conversation, but there are problems with the interpretation of both concepts.

In a quantitative study of discourse features in adult conversations recorded in Glasgow, I found a number of statistically significant differences between males and females. The females used more of the coordinating conjunctions *and* and *but*, and more clauses of reason beginning with *because*. They also used many more pronouns than the males, and in particular the pronoun *she*.

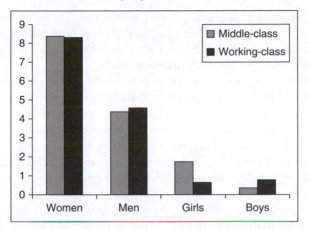

Figure 5.7  Frequency of *you know* in Glasgow (frequency per 1,000 words)

This is probably related to the fact that the women talked more about people, while the men made many more references to places. A greater proportion of the female conversations was taken up with narratives and the narratives contained more examples of dialogue than was the case in the male narratives.

There was also a gender difference in the use of the discourse marker *you know*, as can be seen in the graph shown in Figure 5.7.

Contrary to the view that expressions such as *you know* are more likely to be used by working-class speakers, I found no social class differences but great gender and age differences.

## Understanding variation

Most of the work from sociolinguistic investigations described above falls into the category of correlation studies. In other words, some feature of language is found to co-vary with membership in a social category. Correlation studies, however, do not provide any explanation why some speakers employ a particular form and others do not. In some recent work, sociolinguists have combined quantitative measures with ethnographic description in order to understand what role certain linguistic features play in the particular community. This approach treats the social identity manifested by language as a dynamic process rather than as a passive reflex of a particular status. This is a very promising method and one that marks a return to the way Labov investigated the situation on Martha's Vineyard in his pioneering study.

Carrying out sociolinguistic research is a time-consuming process. Planning the investigation, choosing the sample, recording the speakers, transcribing the tapes or searching them for variables, tabulating the results, and submitting them to statistical analysis: all this takes time and money and a great deal of energy. Despite the success of a number of large-scale surveys and the results of a great many smaller ones, we have only begun to chart the range of variation that can exist in a community and we are a long way from understanding the ways in which speakers can affirm their identity through their speech. There is plenty of opportunity for those who wish to explore this topic further because we have just begun to scratch the surface.

## SUGGESTIONS FOR FURTHER READING

There are quite a few textbooks introducing the field of sociolinguistics: Peter Trudgill *Sociolinguistics*, Suzanne Romaine *Language in Society*, Janet Holmes *An Introduction to Sociolinguistics*, and William Downes *Language and Society*. A wide range of topics is covered in *The Handbook of Language Variation and Change*, edited by J.K.Chambers, Peter Trudgill, and Natalie Schilling-Estes. Good analytical accounts of sociolinguistic studies can be found in J.K. Chambers *Sociolinguistic Theory* and Lesley Milroy and Matthew Gordon *Sociolinguistics: Method and Interpretation*. Sali Tagliamonte gives a good account of sociolinguistic methodology in *Analyzing Sociolinguistic Variation*. Sociolinguistic methodology is also critically evaluated in my *Quantitative Methods in Sociolinguistics*.

The pioneering work of William Labov can be found in *The Social Stratification of English in New York City*, *Language in the Inner City* and *Sociolinguistic Patterns*. Studies following Labov's model include Peter Trudgill *The Social Differentiation of English in Norwich* and my own *Language, Social Class and Education*. The study of Anniston, Alabama is in Crawford Feagin's *Variation and Change in Alabama English*. Nikolas Coupland's *Dialect in Use* reports on a study in Cardiff. Walt Wolfram examines African American speech in *A Sociolinguistic Description of Detroit Negro Speech*. The investigation in Bahia Blanca is reported in Fontanella de Weinberg's *Un Aspecto Sociolinguistico del Español Bonaerense: La –s in Bahia Blanca.* Kevin McCafferty's *Ethnicity and Language Change* describes the situation in Londonderry. *Urban Voices*, edited by Paul Foulkes and Gerard Docherty contains articles on variation in a number of communities including Newcastle. This volume also contains Jane Stuart-Smith's analysis of voice quality in Glasgow. My *Locating Dialect in Discourse* examines the situation in Ayr. Beat Glauser's *The Scottish-English Linguistic Border* examines differences between the language of border Scots and that of their neighbors to the south.

John Rickford's *African American Vernacular English* summarizes a lot of the work on AAVE. Carmen Fought's *Chicano English* and *Language and Ethnicity* deal with Latino English, and the latter also with AAVE and other forms of vernacular English, including Cajun English. Rosina Lippi-Green's *English with an Accent* examines American attitudes to language. The best book on language discrimination is Bonnie Urciuoli's *Exposing Prejudice.*

A good account of American dialects can be found in Walt Wolfram and Natalie Schilling-Estes *American English.* Much information on recent work on regional dialects in the United States can be found in *American Dialect Research* and *Needed Research in American Dialects*, both edited by Dennis Preston. His book *Perceptual Dialectology* summarizes some of his work on folk dialectology. The telephone survey is described in William Labov, Sharon Ash, and Charles Boberg's *The Atlas of North American English.*

The best book on gender differences is Penelope Eckert and Sally McConnell-Ginet's *Language and Gender.* Jennifer Coates in *Women Talk* and *Men Talk* examines gender differences in narrative, while Janet Holmes looks at gender differences in interaction in *Women, Men and Politeness.* The best example of the combination of ethnography and quantitative methods is Penelope Eckert's *Linguistic Variation as Social Practice.* The Glasgow examples from conversations come from my *Talk That Counts.*

# 6

# Language as History

Except for the recent past, where oral history can provide much information, investigating what happened a long time ago is dependent on physical objects. In the case of language the physical objects are examples of writing, preserved on some durable surface. Unfortunately, forms of writing developed relatively late in human development, so we have no evidence of language that goes back more than 6,000 years (see Chapter 7). However, there is general agreement that all known human languages go back to a single origin. Given the nature of language as we understand it, there is no reason to believe that separate groups of our ancestors developed language independently of each other. If they had, languages might differ more fundamentally than is the case with all human languages for which we have any evidence. One of the points on which Chomsky's views have received general acceptance is that all human languages have the same essential features. It is these universal features that make it possible for infants to acquire any language through exposure, regardless of the language of their genetic parents. The same features make it possible to look back in time at unrecorded languages.

## Prehistory

Human beings must have been using language for at least 40,000–60,000 years, the period when the last dispersion from

Africa occurred. Although there are no records of language going back as far as that, there are archaeological findings that provide some information on changes of lifestyle that probably affected language. Recent work on the genetic background of migratory peoples has some interesting findings for language dispersal. Prior to the end of the last major Ice Age, about 15,000 years ago, much of northern and western Europe was covered in ice and was uninhabitable. After the ice receded, there was migration from the Iberian peninsula up the coasts of France and Ireland (which was at this time connected to Great Britain) and round the north of Scotland. These migrants formed the basis of the early population of Brittany, Ireland, Wales, and northwestern Scotland, an area often known at the present day as the Celtic fringe.

About 12,000 years ago, the development of agriculture marks the transition from hunter gatherer societies in the Mesolithic period to communities in the Neolithic period that domesticated some animals and cultivated various crops. The earliest agricultural region was the so-called Fertile Crescent in Mesopotamia, where the climate allowed the cultivation of cereals and pulses. From this location the practice of agriculture and the development of mobile domestic livestock spread eastward into central Asia and the northwest of the Indian subcontinent by about 5000 BC and westward into central Europe by about 4000 BC. In the Yangtze and Yellow River Basins, there is evidence of rice cultivation and domestication of some animals from about 5000 BC. In the Americas, evidence of maize cultivation dates back to at least 3000 BC as does the cultivation of sorghum in Africa. It may not be a coincidence that this division according to four basic foods corresponds roughly to major language families, namely Indo-European, Afroasian, Meso-American, and Sino-Tibetan. There are, however, many more groupings of language families than this global characterization.

The relationship between agriculture and language spread is quite controversial. Some scholars have argued, for example, that Indo-European languages spread out from Anatolia through the peaceful extension of agriculture to neighboring areas rather than by conquest. However, other scholars believe that the dates do not correspond, since some agriculture must have spread at an earlier date than is traditionally given for the dispersion of Indo-European.

The dating of languages before written records depends upon certain assumptions about the rate of change and the attribution of meaning to hypothetical forms. There is also evidence from DNA investigations that is helpful in determining population movements that are relevant to the dispersal of languages, though there is the problem of relating the dispersed peoples to the language they spoke.

## Language reconstruction

> The formation of different languages and of distinct species, and the proofs that both have been developed through a gradual process, are curiously parallel. (Charles Darwin)

There is no direct way of determining the sound or structure of a language for which there are no known records. The best that we can do is work backward from the languages that we know to what plausibly might have preceded them in a kind of reverse history. Instead of charting the changes that have taken place, since we have no direct evidence for them, we reconstruct possible earlier stages of a language that plausibly would have been spoken before any written record. We can do that because of our knowledge of possible sounds and the ways in which they can combine (see Chapter 2), plus other basic elements of linguistic structure. There is no reason to believe that the brains of the earliest speakers were radically different from ours today or that their language was differently structured, though presumably it would have been much less complex, at least in the earlier stages. We also know about the kinds of changes that have occurred in attested languages so that it is reasonable to believe that the same processes would have been operating in pre-historic times.

The first great step in trying to reconstruct an earlier form of language took place in the 19th century. Until the later part of the 18th century interest in older forms of language was concentrated on the classical languages of Latin and Greek and the biblical language of Hebrew. In 1776, Sir William Jones, who had been the chief justice in British India, pointed out that there were interesting resemblances between Sanskrit and European languages such as Latin and Greek. Such resemblances were later investigated by a series of scholars who looked at the forms the word for a common concept might take in putatively related languages and tried to reconstruct a common ancestor for all the cognates (i.e., related forms). This process came to be known as the Comparative Method.

## The comparative method

The Comparative Method operates by examining words with a similar meaning in separate languages to determine whether there are systematic correspondences in the form of the words that suggest a common origin. For example, when traveling in Europe you will find that a feature of many towns is a central square. In France this is a *place*, in Spain it is a *plaza*, in Portugal a *praça*, and in Italy a *piazza*. Since we know from historical records that French, Spanish, Portuguese, and Italian are descendants of the Latin language, we can trace the different forms back to a common ancestor in the Latin *platea* meaning "a broad street." (It may be less obvious that these words are related to the English word *flat*.)

It is not enough, however, to show the relationship among individual words; it is necessary to show that there are systematic differences showing similar relationships among other sets of words. The numerals are an obvious example, though the spelling does not always give a clear indication of differences in pronunciation (Table 6.1).

In the case of these four languages, there are many other words in these languages that show a similar relationship of sounds, so the correspondences are well established. It is also necessary to show that the changes in pronunciation are plausible; that is, the differences must be the result of phonetic processes that have been found to affect linguistic change. Since the time of Sir William Jones, linguists have identified a wide range of types of changes that have occurred in the languages of the world.

## Types of change

### Consonants

There is plenty of evidence of various types of change that have occurred in different languages (Table 6.2). For example, in the process known as **lenition** (i.e., softening) voiceless stops may become voiced, and voiced fricatives may be lost completely. In

**assimilation** two sounds become more similar. Other less frequent changes include reversing the order of sounds **metathesis** and the insertion of a sound **epenthesis**.

Table 6.1    Numbers in four languages descended from Latin

| Latin | Italian | French | Spanish | Portuguese |
|---|---|---|---|---|
| ūnus | uno | un | uno | um |
| duo | due | deux | dos | dois |
| trēs | tre | trios | tres | três |
| quattuor | quattro | quatre | cuatro | quarto |
| quinque | cinque | cinq | cinco | cinco |
| sex | sei | six | seis | seis |
| septem | sette | sept | siete | sete |
| octō | otto | huit | ocho | oito |
| novem | nove | neuf | nueve | nove |
| decem | dieci | dix | diez | dez |
| centum | cento | cent | ciento | cem |

It is not necessary to list all the kinds of changes but there are more than twenty well attested phonetic processes that affect the production of speech sounds and have contributed to linguistic change. Many (but not all) of them can be attributed to what is sometimes called the Principle of Least Effort. Speaking is an effort, as we quickly realize if we are asked to speak at length on any occasion. So it is only natural that speakers should try to minimize this exertion. One way is to use shorter rather than longer words. There is an observation known as Zipf's Law (though it is not a law) that notes that frequently used words tend to be shorter, and there are many examples of shorter versions replacing longer expressions. For example, the first public transport vehicle was known as an *omnibus* (from the Latin "for all," indicating that it was not just for those who could afford to hire a carriage) but it soon became known as a *bus*. In many utterances, the word *television* is replaced by *T.V.*, and so on.

> A struggle for life is constantly going on amongst the words and grammatical forms in each language. The better, the shorter, the easier forms are constantly gaining the upper hand, and they owe their success to their own inherent virtue. (Max Müller)

Table 6.2   Types of sound change

| assimilation | Latin *octo* | → | Italian *otto*. |
|---|---|---|---|
| epenthesis | Old English *botm* | → | Modern English *bottom* |
| | Old Ennglish *ōunor* | → | Modern English *thunder* |
| Lenition | Latin *acqua* | → | Spanish *agua* |
| | Old English *modor* | → | Modern English *mother* |
| | Latin *credere* | → | Spanish *creer* |
| Metathesis | Old English *acsian* | → | Modern English *ask* |
| | Old English *hros* | → | Modern English *horse* |

There is a similar process at work in the articulatory process (Chapter 2). The tongues of speakers move quickly from one position to another and sometimes take short cuts, bringing two sounds closer together, a process known as assimilation, or even omitting sounds at the beginning or end (**apocope**) or middle (**syncope**) of words, and other ways of simplifying articulation. The spelling of words often reflects earlier pronunciations. For example in words such as *knife, knot, gnash,* and *gnaw* the spelling indicates an initial consonant that was once pronounced in earlier forms of English but no longer is. (The development of the present form of orthography for English will be examined in Chapter 7.)

## Vowels

There are also more mysterious changes in the articulation of vowels, which may be shortened or lengthened, raised or lowered, produced further forward in the mouth or further back. As was pointed out in Chapter 2, vowels vary according to the position of the tongue, where the highest part is (nearer the front of the mouth or further back) and how high it is. It is by varying the shape of the resonating chamber that differences in sounds are produced. This is similar to what happens with a musician playing a wind instrument; increasing or decreasing the size of the resonating chamber changes the pitch of the note. Probably one of the factors contributing to changes in the production of vowels is the asymmetry of the mouth.

As the diagram (Figure 6.1) shows, there is more acoustic space at the front of the mouth closer to the teeth, than there is at the back, near the velum. Consequently, there is more acoustic space to keep front vowels distinct than there is for back vowels. If a language

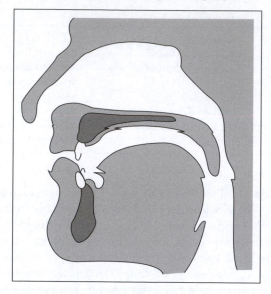

Figure 6.1    Diagram of the mouth

(as frequently but not always happens) has a similar number of front and back vowels, there will be an asymmetry in the system, because the tongue positions for the front vowels will be further apart than those for the back vowels. This makes the system potentially unstable, but not all changes are caused by this asymmetry.

## Neogrammarian hypothesis

> Every sound change, in as much as it occurs mechanically, takes place according to laws that admit no exception. (Hermann Osthoff and Karl Brugmann, 1878)

In the latter part of the 19th century a group of linguists who came to be known as the Neogrammarians claimed that sound change is regular and proceeds without exception. By this they meant that there are changes in certain sounds that have occurred purely through changes in articulation and they maintained that such changes will take place for all the examples of that sound, unless (and this is a big unless) there are other factors that affect the sound in some contexts. The value of this claim was that it forced linguists to look for explanations of apparent counter-examples. One such alternative explanation to regular sound change is the notion of **analogy**. An example of analogical change in morphology is the adoption by many speakers of the past tense form *dove* for the verb *dive*, although the historically attested form is *dived*. The form *dove* is formed on the analogy of such words as *drive/drove* and *strive/ strove*. An example of analogical sound change in English is *chosen*, the past participle of the verb *choose*. In Old English the form was *gecoren*, through a process known as rhotacism whereby the sound [s] becomes [r]. Without analogical change the past participle of *choose* would have been *\*choren*. The result of analogical change is often to make things more regular. Although there are many apparent irregularities in the present-day English verb system for present-day speakers, a conjugation such as *choose/chose/choren* would have been different from anything else. Analogical changes of the kind from *choren* to *chosen*, however, are rare compared with regular sound change and the Neogrammarian hypothesis helped to motivate linguists to investigate all kinds of sound change.

## The notion of "a language"

Linguistic change, however, is not primarily a physiological phenomenon. Social factors are the primary cause of most change in ways of speaking. It is not uncommon to hear people speak of languages changing, even of languages dying, but languages do not change or die. Speakers of the language may change the way in which they speak, and if all the speakers of a language die or stop speaking the language, it will become obsolete and the language will no longer exist as a means of communication, since spoken languages do not have an existence independent of their speakers (except in written records, see Chapter 7).

The tendency to reify languages as independent entities is reinforced by written records (see Chapter 7), but the written form is an inadequate representation of the spoken language. When scholars postulate a common ancestor for cognates in the Romance Languages (French, Italian, Spanish, Portuguese, and so on) the form often does not correspond exactly to the forms that have come down to us in the written records of Latin. The explanation is that the records of what is known as Classical Latin are literary works that generally do not reflect directly the way in which people actually spoke. There are a few examples of what is known as Vulgar Latin (that is, the spoken language) that have survived as graffiti and other forms but they are few in comparison with the records of Classical Latin.

## Evidence of past communities

There are, however, some basic problems with reconstructing proto-languages, that is, languages that are not recorded anywhere but are plausible ancestors of those languages for which we have evidence. As was made clear in Chapter 5, in all societies there is widespread variation in forms of language used. There is no reason to believe that in the period before written records there was no effect of age, gender or social role on the way people spoke. Yet, proto-languages have to be reconstructed as uniform languages because there is no way of hypothesizing the kinds of variation that must have existed.

An even greater problem is that our notion of "a language" is a relatively recent entity closely linked to the concept of national identity. Without a centralized administrative authority there is no need to distinguish between "a language" and "a dialect." There are consequently many problems in working backward through prehistory to postulate "a language" in the modern sense. What can be shown is that many forms in modern languages can be traced back to a common ancestor before the diaspora that led to later differentiations in the ways in which separate communities spoke. This process is useful in two distinct ways. By identifying words of common origin it is possible to gain some idea of the kind of life these ancestors led and thus supplement the evidence from archaeology. The other benefit is that it has encouraged linguists to examine possible forms of sound change that might not otherwise have been noticed.

Nevertheless, the evidence for social and cultural development from presence or absence of vocabulary requires careful evaluation. It is clear from the absence of common words for crops, animals or agricultural activities that the speakers of Khoisan languages in the area around the Kalahari Desert in southern Africa were always hunter-gatherers and never farmers. However, in other situations, the existence of words for domesticated animals in the shared vocabulary of a proto-language may be deceptive because such words could refer to the animals hunted in their wild state.

At one time, attempts to identify the original homeland of the Indo-Europeans were based on the reconstruction of a common form for the beech tree. This was seen as significant because of the (mistaken) belief that beech trees were not to be found east of a line from Kalingrad on the Baltic to Odessa on the Black Sea. Few linguists would now use such an argument. In the first place, it turns out that the area where beech trees were to be found (at the period when the Indo-European language began to split up) was wrongly identified on the basis of the modern distribution of beech trees. More troubling is the discovery that the reconstructed form for the beech refers in some languages to oak trees or even ash trees. In fact, given the difficulty of dealing with meaning in modern languages (see Chapter 1), it is not surprising that there should be uncertainty about the precise reference of reconstructed forms. Moreover, words can change their meaning in totally unpredictable ways. For example, the word *chapel* comes from a word meaning "little cloak," the word *fiasco* means "a bottle" in Italian, and the example of (*omni-*)*bus* given above shows how far an expression meaning "for all" can travel, to use an appropriate metaphor.

*The Oxford English Dictionary (OED)* (also known by its original title *A New English Dictionary on Historical Principles*) provides dates for the earliest occurrence of a word with its presumed meaning. The word *humour* gives a good illustration of the ways in which the meaning of a word can change (Table 6.3).

Table 6.3    Changes in the meaning of the word humor

**Humour > Old French *humor* > Latin *ūmōrem* "fluid, moisture"**

| | |
|---|---|
| 1. moisture, damp exhalation, vapor. | (1382) |
| 2. any fluid or juice of an animal or plant | (1340) |
| 3. one of the four chief fluids of the body: blood, phlegm, choler, melancholy | (1380) |
| 4. with allusion to the mental qualities held to arise from these "humors" | (1475) |
| 5. temporary state of mind or feeling | (1525) |
| 6. particular disposition, inclination, liking | (1565) |
| 7. a) that quality of action, speech or writing which excites amusement b) the faculty of perceiving what is ludicrous or amusing | (1682) |

Medieval medicine held that the "four chief fluids of the body" were responsible for different moods and personality traits, a view that survives in words such as *phlegmatic, choleric,* and *sanguine* (referring to blood).

Despite the problems of dealing with changes in meaning, scholars have done a remarkable job in reconstructing proto-languages for the major language families. One of the most impressive is Proto-Indo-European (PIE) that includes almost all the languages found in present-day Europe. The exceptions are the Uralic languages such as Finnish and Hungarian, and also Basque, which is a language isolate, being unrelated to any other known language.

## Proto-Indo-European (PIE)

The method can be illustrated by the example of the reconstructed PIE form for *pig.* Although wild pigs had been hunted at an earlier period, the domestication of pigs began by the seventh millennium BC in Anatolia and southeast Europe. In Indo-European beliefs the pig is associated with the underworld and the supernatural, and it plays a role in many rituals, particularly those to do with death. The PIE form for "pig" has been reconstructed as **\*sús** based on Latin *sus,* Umbrian *si,* Old Norse *syr,* Old English and Old High German *su,* Albanian *thi,* Greek υς, Avestan *hu,* New Persian *xuk,* Old Indic *sukara,* and Tocharian B *suwo.* It fails to occur only in Armenian and Hittite, but this latter omission may be only accidental since the Hittite word for "pig" is not recorded. The forms in Albanian, Greek, Avestan, and New Persian show a different initial consonant from the others but similar changes are found in other words in these languages, so these are not simply idiosyncratic forms. There is disagreement as to the derivation of the word *\*sús,* with some suggesting that it is from a verb meaning "give birth to" and others that it may simply be the word used to summon pigs. This is the word that appears in English as *sow* and also is the origin of the plural form *swine.* The Modern English word *pig* is of unknown origin and is not found in other Indo-European languages. *Pig* first appears in 13th-century English with the sense of "young pig."

The example of *\*sús* shows how Indo-Europeanists have sifted the evidence from a wide range of languages and come up with a hypothetical ancestor for the words that have been recorded in the different languages. In the course of carrying out this research the scholars also identified the kinds of changes of pronunciation that can take place.

This is a laborious task, much of which was done in the 19th century, and there are now more than 4,000 PIE words that have been reconstructed.

Sometimes a PIE root can appear in different forms in English because of the transmission through other languages (Table 6.4).

Table 6.4  Some English words from the PIE root *pod-

| |
|---|
| foot |
| fetter |
| pew < French |
| pilot < Italian |
| pedestal < Italian |
| pedestrian < Latin |
| podium < Latin |
| pedigree < French |
| peon < Spanish |

## Language families

Whenever Proto-Indo-European was spoken and wherever its original home was, and there is plenty of disagreement about both, there is no disputing that it split up into what are called "language families." These are umbrella terms for groups of related languages (Table 6.5).

Table 6.5  Some Indo-European language families

| | |
|---|---|
| Baltic | Latvian, Lithuanian |
| Celtic | Breton, Gaelic, Irish, Welsh, |
| Germanic | Danish, Dutch, English, German, Norwegian, Swedish |
| Italic | French, Italian, Portuguese, Rumanian, Spanish |
| Slavic | Bulgarian, Polish, Russian, Serb-Croat, Ukranian |
| Indo-Iranian | Farsi, Hindi, Sinhalese |

Germanic is distinguished from its sister branches by what has become known as Grimm's Law, after its discovery by the 19th-century scholar Jakob Grimm. Grimm's Law refers to a series of changes in stop consonants that occurred in the Germanic branch but not in the other branches of Indo-European. The differences can be seen by comparing words in Latin with their equivalents in English (Table 6.6).

Table 6.6    Examples of Grimm's Law

| Latin | English |
|-------|---------|
| pedem | foot |
| tres | three |
| cordem | heart |

These examples illustrate the changes [p] > [f], [t] > [θ], and [k] > [h]. There were other changes that need not be illustrated here but the main point is that Grimm's Law applied across a wide range of examples so that it is no surprise that, for example, Latin *pisces* should correspond to English *fish* and Latin *centum* to English *hundred*, and so on.

## Old English

The process of reconstruction is often hampered by lack of adequate information about earlier stages of the languages. The survival of written records is often a matter of luck and there is much more information about some languages than others. In the case of English we are fortunate to have extensive written materials that date back to the 8th century. We are particularly indebted to King Alfred (849–899), who strongly believed in the value of writing in education and had the political means to encourage the production and dissemination of manuscripts. As a result we have much more information on Old English (sometimes called Anglo-Saxon) than exists for any other Germanic language, and we can chart the changes that have taken place over the past 1500 years.

Unfortunately, however, we do not have a complete picture of how Old English actually sounded. This is because most of the materials that have survived were written in a standardized orthography that does not reflect some changes that were taking place in the spoken language toward the end of the Old English period. The problems are less with the consonants because there are fewer changes to investigate but some of the representations of vowels are difficult to interpret. Despite these difficulties, scholars have been able to create a plausible trajectory for the development of the Old English system into its later manifestations. Numerous phonetic processes, such as the fronting, unrounding, lengthening, and shortening of vowels took place between the later Old English period (circa 1000 AD) and the early Middle English period (circa 1200 AD). The changes are too complex to illustrate here but they explain such pairs as *fox/vixen* and *mouse/mice* where what was originally the same vowel has split into two contrasting forms as the result of regular phonetic processes. (The occurrence of [v] in *vixen* is a rare survival of a western dialect form.)

Although there are still many points on which scholars disagree, the overall picture of the changes in pronunciation from Old English times to the present is not in dispute. The major disagreements are about when and how the changes occurred. Some changes, however, are limited to specific areas of the country. For example, in the 17th century the vowel in words such as *cut, duck, mud,* and *sun* which until then had been a rounded vowel (similar to that in *bush* and *pull*) changed to the unrounded vowel that is used today in most dialects. This change, however, affected only the southern half of England. In the northern part, the rounded vowel continued to be used. Slightly later, the vowel in words such as *staff, large,* and *glass* lengthened in the south creating a contrast in words such as *psalm* and *Sam.* Again this change did not occur in the north.

In recent years more attention has been paid to linguistic variation (see Chapter 5) in historical studies as well as contemporary ones. Older accounts of the changes in pronunciation emphasized those changes that were (or seemed to be) heading in the direction of the present-day prestige form. This had the effect of diverting attention from the less prestigious varieties. Since in contemporary England only a small minority of the population use the prestige form, **Received Pronunciation (RP)** as it is called, much of the information relating to the majority of speakers was ignored. For example, what is known as "h-dropping," that is, the omission of the initial consonant in words such as *house* and *hope,* is generally stigmatized in England, and is considered to be a sign of working-class speech. It has been shown, however, that there is a long history of h-dropping in England, though traditional histories of the language tended to ignore this. It is likely that future historical linguists will be more interested in exploring the kinds of variation that sociolinguists have found in modern societies.

## Corpus-based studies

The study of language change has been assisted in the latter part of the 20th century by the existence of the digital computer. This has made possible the development of computerized corpora of older texts. Before the invention of computers many hard-working scholars searched through texts to trace changes, but this was a labor-intensive procedure that took time. Computers have not changed the process, but they have made it quicker and easier. Since it is a simple task to search for forms on the computer, scholars can track the frequency with which an item occurs in the texts. One of the earliest corpora is the Helsinki Corpus of English Texts, which consists of approximately 1.5 million words from the period 850–1710. The Helsinki Corpus contains about four hundred samples of texts from such sources as legal documents, scientific works, sermons and religious treatises, the Bible, philosophical and historical works, travel and autobiographical writings, drama, private and official letters, and diaries. The variety is least for the earlier periods but in the Late Middle English and Early Modern English periods there are examples from different kinds of texts. For the later periods it has been possible for the compilers to include information on the age, sex, and social position of the writers, and in the case of letters to specify the relationship between the writer and the person to whom the letter is addressed. This often makes it possible to examine the distribution of variants in much the same way as a contemporary sociolinguistic study.

One example will illustrate the possibilities. In present-day English the present perfect form of the verb usually consists of the auxiliary *have* plus the past participle of the verb, as in *he has gone to China*. At an earlier stage of the language the verb *go* formed its present perfect with the auxiliary *be*. This may still be heard in situations such as a death scene in which someone says *he is gone*. (Of course, with the contracted form of the auxiliary in *he's gone* it is impossible to say whether it is *be* or *have*.) Originally, *have* was used only with transitive verbs, for example, *he has bought a house* and *be* was used with intransitive verbs, for example, *they are arrived*. This distinction continued until the 18th century when *be* was gradually replaced by *have*. The latest to change over to *have* were verbs that indicated a change of state, for example, *grow, become, wax*. All this was known from earlier studies but a search of the computerized corpus provided more information about how this change took place. The use of *have* for all perfects was not dominant in drama or fiction until the 19th century, but it was well established in journals and letters by the 18th century. Although the evidence is fragile because of the small number of texts, it appears that in the period 1350–1500 women were in the vanguard in adopting the new *have* form. However, in the period 1700–1900 women are more likely than men to use the traditional *be* form. The corpora on which these conclusions are based consist of samples of language from the various periods. Given the speed with which computerization has proceeded, it is likely that these corpora will be superseded by larger and better collections, and this may change the results. There are also problems with the classification of texts into genres. Some genres such as sermons and private letters may be relatively coherent, but genres such as fiction and travel writing are very broad. Nevertheless, it is likely that computerized corpora will play an increasing role in the study of many kinds of language change.

## Grammaticalization

One of the topics that has received increased attention in recent years is the process known as grammaticalization. This is a process where a linguistic form (usually a word) loses some of its meaning while taking on a new function. This can be illustrated by the verb *go* (Table 6.7).

Table 6.7   The grammaticalization of the word *go*

a. I am going to London on the train
b. I am going to buy it
c. I am going to like it
d. It is going to rain
e. I'm going to go there tomorrow
f. I'm gonna go today
g. She goes "They're not my relatives"

In (a) the meaning of *go* clearly indicates motion, but this sense is absent from the other examples, and in (g) has lost any implication of intention or future. (In fact, (g) is an example of a Conversational Historical Present, in which the present tense is used in a narrative to refer to an event in the past.) *Be going to* has become a pseudo-auxiliary equivalent to the modal auxiliary *will*. This replicates the development of the modal auxiliaries from their Old English forms. The Old English ancestors of words such as *can* and *must* were different from other verbs in many ways but they were able to take a direct object. By the 15th century this was no longer possible and the class of modal auxiliaries was established.

Grammaticalization often results in a linguistic form changing its role in the system. At one time linguists drew a distinction between **Content Words** and **Function Words.** Content words are words for objects, actions, qualities, and so on, represented in the lexicon by nouns, verbs, and adjectives that have a paraphrasable meaning. Function words express relational concepts and consist of forms such as auxiliaries, some prepositions and conjunctions whose meaning are harder to express concisely. (There is some experimental evidence to suggest that content words and function words are differently stored in the brain, and this would reinforce the value of such a classification.) More recent views have characterized Noun, Verb, Adjective and Preposition as lexical categories in contrast to the functional categories of Determiner, Auxiliary, and Intensifier. Lexical categories can take full stress while functional categories are lightly stressed, unless for emphasis. Though the distinction has its problems, it may help to explain the process of grammaticalization in which lexical categories lose some of their meaning (a process sometimes known as **bleaching**) and are likely to show reduced stress. This can be seen in the reduction of *going to* to *gonna* and in the contraction of *indeed* from "in deed" (i.e, in action) and *instead* from "in stead" (i.e., in place). There are also cases where the meaning has changed radically as in *handicap* from "hand in cap" (a lottery game in which forfeits were held in a cap). The development of the discourse markers *you know, I mean*, and *I think*, which are usually lightly stressed, is another example of grammaticalization.

Table 6.8   Some examples of grammaticalization

| on way | → | away |
|---|---|---|
| on sleep | → | asleep |
| on live | → | alive |
| on by outside | → | about |
| by sides | → | besides |
| by cause | → | because |
| all one | → | alone |
| in stede ("place") | → | instead |
| in deed | → | indeed |

It is not a coincidence that grammaticalization has become an interesting topic in recent years since it coincides with the emphasis on functional approaches to the study of syntax. Formal syntacticians (see Chapter 3) were not interested in processes such as grammaticalization because their model is of a static system. From this perspective, changes do not occur in languages but in grammars. Since the grammar in the formalist model is a representation of the speaker's competence and it is assumed not to change after the initial acquisition, there is no way to incorporate a process such as grammaticalization. In a dynamic model of the kind proposed by many functionalists (see Chapter 3), the system is believed to be fluid and able to adapt to changes. In fact, some functionalists have used the term **emergent grammar** to describe the situation. Once again, the polarization between the formalists and the functionalists is obvious.

## Investigating change in progress

Another area that has received much attention in recent years is what William Labov has labeled "the use of the present to explain the past." This is the notion that by studying how language is changing at the present time we may be better able to understand changes that have occurred in the past. Underlying this approach is the **uniformitarian principle,** taken over from geology, which states that the processes that operate now must be the same as those that operated in the past. Since, as pointed out earlier, there is no reason to believe that the physiological basis of language has changed, similar kinds of changes in articulation are likely to have occurred in the past.

Recent technological developments have made possible the analysis of the kinds of changes in pronunciation that are taking place at the present time. The first is the high quality battery operated tape recorder that can be used to collect the examples of spontaneous speech that are crucial for tracking possible changes. The second is the development of a sociolinguistic methodology that allows the systematic investigation of speech variation in the community (see Chapter 5). The third is the improvement in techniques for the acoustic analysis of speech (Chapter 2) that now can be carried out on digitalized samples on the computer. It has been claimed that this instrumental analysis provides a more objective view than can be achieved by listening to the tapes, though there are also some fundamental problems with this method. The major one is that speakers have different sized mouths and this affects the formant values of vowels that sound the same when spoken by men compared with women or adults compared with children. There are methods of normalizing the speech sample to compensate for the physical differences, though some scholars remain skeptical about the normalizing procedures.

One of the problems in studying change in progress is that there are only a few cases with comparable evidence from even twenty or thirty years ago. An alternative to examining speech samples from different periods (known as **real-time studies**) is to collect samples from people of different ages and chart what differences there are between younger and older speakers (**apparent-time studies**). By tabulating an increase (or decrease) in the use of a variant by younger speakers the investigator can explore the possibility that this represents a change in progress. There could, of course, be another explanation. It is well-known that adolescents often adopt forms of speech that they will abandon later as they mature, so differences from the speech of their elders may not give a true indication of their later language. There have, however, been a few studies where trends indicated in an apparent-time study have been confirmed by a later "real-time" investigation, and this has reinforced confidence in some of the results of apparent-times studies.

The leading investigator of change in progress has been William Labov and one of his greatest successes has been the identification of what he called the Northern Cities Shift in the United States. The series of changes that began in the middle of the 20th century affect in a uniform way the vast area of the Inland North, stretching from Madison, Wisconsin to Syracuse, New York. The Northern Cities Shift is an example of a **chain shift**. In a chain shift a number of sounds (usually vowels) change position so that while (generally) maintaining distance from each other end up in somewhat different locations. The best known example of a chain shift is what is known as the **Great Vowel Shift** which took place in English some time between the death of Chaucer in 1400 and Shakespeare's lifetime.

What happened was that in a word such as *name* that was pronounced with a low front vowel [æ:] (like a long version of the vowel in *cat*) the vowel was raised to be [e:] as in present-day pronunciation while the vowel in a word such as *meat*, which had been pronounced like present-day *mate* was raised to its present-day sound, similar to *meet*. Meanwhile, a word such as *mite*, which had been till then pronounced like present-day *meet* was shunted down to become a diphthong as in its present day pronunciation. A similar process occurred with the back vowels. These changes seem to have happened at the same time, although there is disagreement as to when and how they occurred. There were other changes going on at the same time but this brief account may serve to give an indication of a chain shift. It is generally thought of as a push chain, on the assumption that the articulation of the vowel in words such as *mate* began to move higher in the mouth and this caused the articulation of the vowel in words such as *meat* to move higher in order to maintain the distinction from the vowel in words such as *mate*, and so on.

In the contemporary Northern Cities Shift in the United States what seems to have happened is that there was a change in the pronunciation of the back vowels in words such as *caught* and *cot*. In accounts of American English until recently, these vowels have been listed as being distinct. However, one of the major changes that has been taking place in recent years (not only in the Inland North) has been a tendency for these two words (and others like them) to be pronounced the same. This is a change that has been well documented over the past few years (see Chapter 5). This may not have been the driving force for the Northern Cities Shift but something affected the pronunciation of words with the low front vowel [æ] in words such as *can*, *camp*, and *bag*. In extreme examples of the change this vowel is pronounced similar to the [i:] vowel in *keen*. In fact, one couple who had named their son Ian was accused of having given him a girl's name because the hearer equated the sound with that of the name Ann. The Northern Cities Shift began in Western New England and then moved west through Pennsylvania, Ohio, Illinois, and Michigan, and particularly affected younger speakers in the cities of Buffalo, Cleveland, Detroit, and Chicago.

## Social factors in change

In addition to looking at the kind of physiological factors that can affect sound change, such as chain shifts, Labov has also investigated the social conditions that may influence change. His general thesis is that in a socially stratified society the impetus for change is likely to come from the lower middle-class or upper working-class groups. Moreover, women tend to lead in these changes, but men follow on a generation later, influenced no doubt by their mothers. These claims are tentative, based on the evidence Labov has collected from his very extensive investigations and careful analysis of the materials, and they remain as hypotheses to be tested by future studies. But anyone who wishes

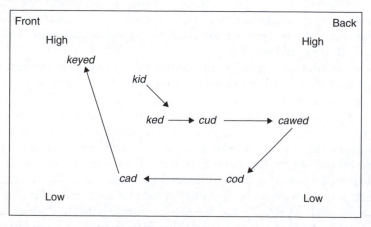

Figure 6.2   The Northern Cities Shift

to challenge Labov's views will have to carry out equally rigorous investigations.

Other scholars have shown how membership in **social networks** or **communities of practice** can affect speakers' involvement in ongoing changes. Such groupings can include gang membership or belonging to a high school category such as "jocks" (those who participate fully in the school culture) and "burnouts" (those who rebel against the school's values and orient themselves more to the adult world outside the school).

There are many complex factors that affect how people speak (Chapter 5) and any of them can also influence changes. It is undeniable that there are always changes taking place in language. The most obvious is in vocabulary where inventions and procedures require labels, but there can also be changes in the way speakers use words and expressions (e.g., *hopefully, like*). Changes in pronunciation are more subtle and may not be obvious to the speakers themselves. At the same time, there is great continuity in a language and some very common words in English may not have changed their pronunciation much in over 1500 years. It is perhaps a paradox that language is both dynamic and remarkably stable.

## SUGGESTIONS FOR FURTHER READING

Works dealing with the historical development of English show a distressing tendency to begin with the most indigestible part, namely Old English. By the time you have struggled through declensions and conjugations and seven types of verb classes you may feel you have blundered into a work on German grammar. Welcome exceptions are Jeremy Smith's *An Historical Study of English* and Dick Leith's *A Social History of English*. For the more typical approach, a good place to start is N.F. Blake's a *History of the English Language,* though my advice is to skim over the section on Old English as quickly as possible and get to late Middle English around the time of Chaucer. From then on, reading will be much easier. Two very readable books that do not require linguistic training are Owen Barfield's *History in English Words* and Raymond Williams' *Keywords.* Both show how many words that we use frequently at present had different senses in the past.

Labov's pioneering work on linguistic is presented in *The Social Stratification of English in New York City,* supplemented by *Sociolinguistic Patterns* and *Language in the Inner City.* His later work is contained in the two monumental volumes entitled *Principles of Linguistic Change*, the first dealing with "Internal Factors" and the second with "Social factors." Neither is easy reading, even for those familiar with the field, but they contain a vast amount of valuable analysis and discussion. Some of the evidence for the Northern Cities Shift and other changes can be found in William Labov, Sharon Ash and Charles Boberg's *Atlas of North American English*, based on telephone interviews with 762 speakers from all the urban areas across the United States.

The dispersal of language families is examined in an interesting volume edited by Peter Bellwood and Colin Renfrew *Examining the Farming/ Language Dispersal Hypothesis*. The genetic background is explored even more fully in Stephen Oppenheimer's *The Origins of the British*. A vast store of information on Indo-European languages and culture can be found in J.P. Mallory and D.Q. Adams *Encyclopedia of Indo-European Culture*.

The question of when h-dropping began is examined in James Milroy *Linguistic Variation and Change*. The account of *be/have* + past participle comes from an article by Merja Kytö in *English in Transition* edited by Matti Rissanen, Merja Kytö, and Kirsi Heikkonen. Examples of grammaticalization can be found in Laurel J. Brinton and Elizabeth Closs Traugott *Lexicalization and Language Change*. The contrast between "jocks" and "burnouts" is described in Penelope Eckert's *Linguistic Variation as Social Practice,* a careful study of change in a Detroit high school, combining ethnographic and quantitative methods in an innovative fashion, and showing the importance of social networks and communities of practice. Lesley Milroy's study of Belfast speech *Language and Social Networks* was the first sociolinguistic study to show the significance of social networks.

# 7

# Language as Symbol

As pointed out in Chapter 6, we have no clear idea of how long human beings have been speaking something that we would consider language, because there are no records going back more than six thousand years. We do, however, have written records from about 3000 B.C. and we can trace the development of writing systems from then until the present. Writing systems evolved from early forms of record-keeping that used iconic representations of physical objects. The first scripts to go beyond record-keeping are all pictographic, that is, the symbols represented objects such as a tree or the moon as well as referring to important individuals. It was therefore possible to create narratives using these symbols. This iconic system, however, is severely limited to those messages that can be unambiguously recognized from the symbols. It also requires a very large stock of symbols, since they must be distinct from each other. The need to make the system more flexible led to the stylization of the pictorial symbols. As a result, the symbols could no longer be interpreted solely on the basis of their form. It had become necessary to learn the script.

There are similarities between the earliest writing systems and the use of iconic signs on roads. Some of these are obvious from their images, as in the examples in the first line, but others are arbitrary in relation to their meaning and need to be learned, as in the examples in the second line (Figure 7.1).

As the early writing systems lost their iconic meaning, they became more like the second line of symbols.

Figure 7.1    Iconic and non-iconic road signs

## Sumerian cuneiform

The earliest script that is a direct ancestor of alphabetic writing is Sumerian **cuneiform,** of which there are examples dating back to 3000 BC. Over the next thousand years the Sumerian system evolved, not by adding symbols, but by reducing the number in common use from about 2,000 to 500. The reason for this reduction is obviously to do with memory limitations. Sumerian cuneiform is a logographic system, which means that each symbol represents a word that has to be committed to memory. **Logographic** systems have the advantage of being easy to read but the disadvantage of being hard to acquire. The Chinese writing system is logographic and an 18th century dictionary lists almost 50,000 characters. At the present time it has been claimed that about 1,000 characters are enough to represent most of the material in current Chinese publications. This is still a lot to commit to memory.

## Syllabic systems

A system that places less strain on the memory than a logographic one is a script that represents syllables rather than words. This reduces the number of symbols that have to be learned. A syllabic writing system has a symbol for each syllable, such as *pa, ta,* and *ka* but no separate symbols for *p, t, k* or *a.* This type of system works best with languages that have a relatively simple syllable structure, preferably one in which most syllables consist of a single consonant followed by a vowel. It does not work well for a language such as English, which has initial consonant clusters of up to three consonants as in *straw* and up to four consonants in final position as in *sixths*. For English and for the majority of languages an **alphabetic writing system**, in which each sound has its symbol, is the most economical because only a relatively small set of symbols is required. The Roman alphabet, which became the script for languages such as English, French, Spanish, and many others, takes its origin from the Semitic script of Phoenician.

## Alphabetic systems

Because of the structure of Semitic languages, in which most words have roots consisting of two or three consonants, Semitic scripts did not need to represent the vowels. When the Greeks adopted the Phoenician script for their own purposes, they adapted some of the symbols to represent vowels. There is some dispute as to when the Greeks first began to use the new system, but around 1000 BC is one suggested date. Whenever it was, the Greeks were the first to develop an alphabetic system of writing in which the sounds in the words were represented by separate symbols. The Roman alphabet is a direct descendant of the Greek system. There are many other alphabetic scripts and the Roman alphabet would not win many prizes for its aesthetic qualities. Like the Romans as a people, it is efficient and functional, but not focused on beauty. There are many scripts that are simply a delight to look at. An emperor's name on a ceramic panel in Arabic script can be a work of art. Many scripts on the Indian subcontinent are very elegant, and the Han'gul script created in the 15th century by the Korean king Sejong is both a very dramatic and effective script.

Alphabetic scripts are highly valued because they are an effective way of representing most types of languages, but there are two exceptions. One is where it is necessary to indicate **lexical tone**, that is, where words with the same sequence of sounds are distinguished by the pitch with which they are uttered: high, low, rising or falling. The other case is a language that has a large number of **homophones**, that is, words with the same sequence of sounds but different meanings. Since both conditions are true of Chinese, it is not surprising that Chinese is written in a logographic script.

Chomsky once illustrated the phenomenon of homophony in English with the pair of utterances *the sun's rays meet* and *the sons raise meat*. (A similar example from French is *elle se lève toujours a cette heure* "she always gets up at this time" and *elle se lève toujours a sept heures* "she always gets up at seven o'clock.") In speech, homophones seldom cause problems, though they may elicit groans when used as puns. In writing, however, distinguishing homophones may make it easier to comprehend the text more quickly. At one time there was a phonetics journal *Le Maitre Phonetique* which was published using the International Phonetic Alphabet. Although the readers were fully competent in using the phonetic symbols, it was extremely tedious to read and eventually the journal changed to normal orthography.

---

ðə jus əv fənɛtɪk sɪmbəɪz šoz hau wi spik ðo ɪt ɪznt izi tə rid
"The use of phonetic symbols shows how we speak though it isn't easy to read"

---

## Standard languages

An orthography (literally "correct writing," i.e., spelling) is a system that sets a standard form for representing a language, so orthographies are established and maintained by official policy. This has many consequences for the speakers of the language. For one thing, it creates a measure of correctness, not only for writing but also for what is considered to be the standard language. There are two distinct senses of the word *standard*. One is the sense of setting a model for imitation, as in a standard weight or measurement. The other is the notion of average, as a standard size in contrast to larger or smaller. The expression **Standard English** clearly implies the first sense, since it is never used to refer to the language of the majority but to that of the educated elite. The kind of language that sociolinguists refer to as the vernacular (see Chapter 5) is the language of the majority but it does not have the prestige of Standard English. When there is concern about some nonstandard variety, as happened with the Ebonics crisis in

Oakland (see Chapter 5), the comparison is always with Standard English, which is assumed to be superior. Many people believe that Standard English is the best possible form of English because it is: (1) the most logical, (2) the most regular, and (3) the most beautiful. None of these claims is valid.

Standard English is the result of a process that established a convention as to the correct form in which to write serious prose. The creators of this convention include the dictionary makers and the editors of major newspapers and publishers. Consequently, there are different standards in Britain and the United States, though the differences are relatively minor. These printed materials provide the model from which all notions of correctness in language are drawn. In the case of English, we are able to track the route by which this standard language evolved. We are able to do this because we have written records for more than a thousand years, starting with the Old English period (see Chapter 6).

## Scribal practices

When the Germanic tribes first began to settle in Britain in the 5th century AD, there was considerable dialect variation because the tribes came from different regions on the continent. By the 7th century, if not before, there were four distinct dialect areas in England that have been identified by later scholars. The Kentish kingdom, in the southeast was dominant to begin with, followed in turn by Mercian, in the Midlands, and Northumbrian, in the north, and finally, West Saxon, in the southwest. Each dialect was written in a form slightly different from the others.

The labels corresponded to regions of political power and over two centuries, the dominance shifted from Kent northwards until in the 9th century the power shifted south again and the West Saxon Kingdom (Wessex), under King Alfred, became the dominant region. Through Alfred's influence, scriptoria (writing centers) were established and all existing earlier manuscripts including those in other dialects were copied in the West Saxon dialect. Thus, our knowledge of Old English, with a few exceptions, is based mainly on these West Saxon materials.

One of the exceptions is the Ruthwell Cross that dates from the 7th century. On it are carved parts of the Old English poem known as *The Dream of the Rood* (i.e., the Cross). The carving is in the

Runic alphabet, a form of writing used by the Germanic tribes mainly to record names (Figure 7.2).

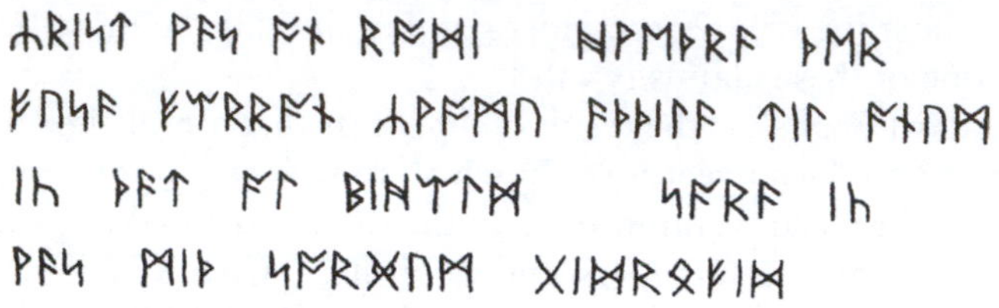

ᚪᚱᛁᛋᛏ ᛈᚳᛋ ᚱᛏ ᚱᚩᚻᛁ   ᚾᛈᛗᚻᚱᚠ ᚻᛗᚱ
ᚠᚢᛋᚠ ᚠᛇᚱᚱᚠᛏ ᚪᛈᚠᛗᚾ ᚠᚻᚻᛁᚠᚠ ᛏᛁᚠ ᚠᛏᚢᛗ
ᛁᚻ ᚻᚠᛏ ᚠᚠ ᛒᛁᚾᛇᚻ   ᛋᚠᚱᚠ ᛁᚻ
ᛈᚳᛋ ᛗᛁᚻ ᛋᚠᚱᛉᚢᛗ ᚷᛁᛗᚱᛟᚠᛁᛗ

Figure 7.2   Example of Runic writing

The Runic characters represent the Old English text:

> Crist wæs on rode
> Hwæðere ðær fuse feorran cwome
> to ðam Æðelinge ic ðæt eall behold
> Sare ic wæs mid sorgum gedrefed

The cross is speaking and it can be translated as:

Christ was on the cross. Thither they came hurrying from afar to the Lord. I saw all that. I was sorely troubled with grief.

There are, however, few extended Old English texts written in the Runic script.

## West Saxon scriptoria

The West Saxon scribes were monks who worked together in writing centers known as **scriptoria**. They developed an orthography that represented the language in a consistent way, but it does not give as comprehensive a guide to the spoken language as we would like. We know this because of the political upheaval that followed the defeat of the West Saxon king by William of Normandy in 1066. Following this defeat, the Anglo-Saxon administrators were replaced by William's French-speaking supporters, and for about three hundred years, French was the official language at the royal court, though the majority of the population continued to speak a form of English. During this period the West Saxon tradition of writing in English was lost and a new conventional form had to be developed, but this did not happen for about four centuries.

The West Saxon orthography had been adapted from Latin, since the scribes belonged to the church, though there were a few modifications added to represent sounds that did not occur in Latin. For the most part, it is relatively easy to interpret the West Saxon spellings, though there are certain representations of vowels that have remained problematic. After the Normans assumed power, the scriptoria continued to produce manuscripts written in standard West Saxon, but gradually the tradition was lost, and later scribes, who had not been trained in the old orthography, began to write down what they heard. The scriptoria in the monasteries were taken over by French-speaking scribes who were not trained in the Old English system. This mattered less than it might have done because almost all important documents were written in French or Latin. English was not used as the language of administration, so there was no need for a standardized written form.

## Written Middle English

When scribes who had not been trained in the West Saxon system later began to write English they adopted new conventions, some of them borrowed from French, but there was no standardized system. Thus, for a period in the history of English (c.1100–1350) we have manuscripts that give much more information about details of pronunciation than earlier or later writings, since the scribes were trying to represent what they heard. The early Middle English manuscripts are thus particularly useful for understanding some of the changes in pronunciation that must have already taken place in West Saxon. This information about changes in pronunciation has survived because there was no longer any standard orthography for writing English in the 12th century. The scribes were free to develop their own ways of representing sounds and this led to a great variety. Moreover, there were many local variations in the grammar, vocabulary, and pronunciation of the texts, and the manuscripts provide a record of this variation that is much richer than anything we have for the Old English period. From these materials, however, we can identify some of the sound changes that must have occurred in the Old English period but were not reflected in the manuscripts written in standard West Saxon orthography. We know this because the language could not have changed so fundamentally and rapidly in the period between the last West Saxon manuscripts and the earliest Middle English texts.

## The emergence of Standard English

Various early Middle English texts provide a range of different approaches to the problem of writing in English. By Chaucer's time (c.1340–1400), a conventional system was beginning to emerge in court circles around London but there was still plenty of variety elsewhere in the country. The most impressive documentation of the great variety in spelling that existed outside of the London area is in a four-volume set entitled *A Linguistic Atlas of Late Mediaeval English (LALME)*. This work covers the period 1350–1450, from the resurgence of English as a written language in the middle of the 14th century till the adoption of a standard form of writing, known as Chancery English, in the later part of the 15th century. Chancery English was the form of spelling adopted for use in government documents and it became the basis for the development of later orthographies. The need for standardization can be understood from the wealth of different spellings recorded in *LALME*. There are over 60 spellings of the word *her*, over 100 of *they*, 120 variants of the word *be* and almost 500 different spellings of the words *through* and *(al-)though*. The editors of *LALME* were able to identify different scribes by their idiosyncratic spellings and often were able to locate the place where the scribe learned to write, identifying it to within a radius of ten miles. *LALME* is one of the most impressive works of scholarship dealing with variation in writing. By the end of the 15th century, however, the introduction of the printing press was instrumental in establishing a national standard for spelling, based on Chancery English.

## Impact of printing

The adoption of printing had a powerful impact on the development of a written standard. Medieval manuscripts had to be laboriously copied by hand and scribes not only occasionally made errors, but they also sometimes took it upon themselves to "correct" forms that they considered to be wrong. The manuscripts were also often prepared for specific patrons, so the scribe could take that into account in preparing the document. (A number of the Old English works that have survived were composed in a dialect different from West Saxon, but the copies we have are in the West Saxon dialect of the scribes and their patrons.) Scribal flexibility when copying manuscripts changed completely with the invention of printing, since multiple copies could be produced for widespread distribution. It is a significant coincidence that the introduction of printing in England happened at a time when the conventional form of spelling had more or less stabilized to the form in which it has continued to the present day (though there were many minor differences). The production of printed texts rather than manuscripts, however, did not immediately lead to unanimity in spelling. Printers in Shakespeare's time would use different spellings of words in order to shorten or lengthen a line of print, a practice known as "justifying" the line to give the page a regular appearance. The following is an example from the first quarto edition of *Hamlet*.

*Ham.* To be, or not to be, that is the queſtion,
Whether tis nobler in the minde to ſuffer
The ſlings and arrowes of outragious fortune,
Or to take Armes againſt a ſea of troubles,
And by oppoſing, end them, to die to ſleepe
No more, and by a ſleepe, to ſay we end
The hart-ake, and the thouſand naturall ſhocks
That fleſh is heire to; tis a conſumaticn
Deuoutly to be wiſht to die to ſleepe,
To ſleepe, perchance to dreame, I there's the rub,
For in that ſleepe of death what dreames may come
When we haue ſhuffled off this mortall coyle
Muſt giue vs pauſe, there's the reſpect
That makes calamitie of ſo long life:

It was only in the 18th century that strict conformity with established standards of spelling became the norm for printed texts. (Private letters, however, continued to show variation in spelling.)

## English orthography

The way English is now spelled has not changed radically from
the form used in the late 15th century, though the spoken language has undergone some major changes. This conservatism
is possible because of the type of orthography that was developed. Some languages are written in what has been called a
"shallow" orthography in which the symbols closely represent
the pronunciation. No writing system provides the exact correspondence between sound and symbol that the International
Phonetic Alphabet (IPA) does, but many languages have a system
that keeps close to the distinctions made in speaking. Spanish is
a good example of this. English orthography is at the opposite
extreme from this, as is French. The economist Thorstein Veblen
cited the conventional spelling of English as an example of conspicuous consumption.

> " As felicitous an instance of futile classicism as can well be found, outside of
> the Far East, is the conventional spelling of the English language. A breach
> in the proprieties in spelling is extremely annoying and will discredit any
> writer in the eyes of all persons who are possessed of a developed sense
> of the true and beautiful. (Thorstein Veblen)

The aim of a phonetic transcription is to have each symbol
uniquely correspond to one sound, so the IPA phonetic symbol [s]
always represents the sound at the beginning of the word *sing* or
the end of *cats*. In English orthography that is not the case, since
the letter *s* corresponds not only to the sound [s] in *cats,* but aso to
the sound [z] in *dogs* and to the sound [š] in *sugar.* Even more con-
fusingly, the letter *s* occurs in combination with other letters to
represent the sound [š], as in *ship, tension, mission, luscious,* and
*tissue.* There are twelve different ways to represent one English
vowel as shown in the words *seem, he, meat, receive, believe,
discrete, Caesarian, people, amoeba, machine, key,* and *quay.*
Despite this, English orthography has been called an optimal system for writing English. The explanation is that once we have
mastered the system it works extremely well. Take, for example,
the final *e* that distinguishes the vowels in *fat* and *fate, pet* and
*Pete, sit* and *site, nod* and *node, jut* and *jute.* This 'silent *e*' is not
pronounced but it serves to distinguish the preceding vowel. It can

also change the consonant as in *rag* vs. *rage*. Once we have understood the value of the "silent e," we would be able to pronounce
new words, such as *\*dit* and *\*dite* (even though the spell-checker
rejects them).

There are also systematic vowel and consonant differences
between related words, such as *sane* and *sanity*, *extreme* and
*extremity*, *wide* and *width*, and *phone* and *phonic*. These vowel
differences are the result of the Great Vowel Shift (Chapter 6) that
raised the long (tense) vowels in words such as *sane, extreme,* and
so on, but in words such as *sanity* and *extremity* the corresponding
vowel was shortened (for predictable reasons) and the short vowels
were not raised. A spelling system that used a different symbol for
the vowels in *sane* and *sanity* (i.e., a more phonetic one) would
obscure the relationship between the two words.

There are similar kinds of systematic differences in consonants
between related words, as in *medical* vs. *medicine, race* vs. *racial,
resident* vs. *residential, revise* vs. *revision, democratic* vs. *democ-
racy,* and *prodigal* vs. *prodigious*. There are also "silent" letters
that are pronounced in related words, as in *malign* vs. *malignant,
condemn* vs. *condemnation,* and *muscle* vs. *muscular*. All these
spellings make the words easier to recognize in reading. There are
also words that sound the same but are spelled differently, as *site,
cite* and *sight* or *meat, mete,* and *meet*. The survival of initial consonants that are no longer pronounced help to distinguish *knot*
from *not* and *wrap* from *rap*.

There are, however, a number of irregular spellings that are more
confusing: *one, two, bread, steak, come, thorough, bough, cough*
and quite a few others. They simply have to be learned as exceptions to the general spelling rules. Another potential source of confusion comes from **homographs**, that is, words that are spelled the
same way, but are pronounced differently. Examples are the noun
*tear* and the verb *tear,* or the noun *wind* and the verb *wind* (as in
wind up a clock). In practice, there are few of these homographs
and they seldom cause problems since they occur in different syntactic contexts.

English orthography has the form it does because it preserves
features of the spoken language from the past that are no longer observed. For example, the difference in spelling between the
homophones *meet* and *meat* reflects a difference in pronunciation at an earlier period, when the tongue position for the vowel

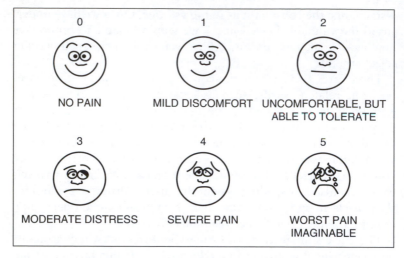

Figure 7.3    Iconic symbols for degrees of pain

in *meat* was lower in the mouth than for the vowel in *meet*. Somewhere around the 17th century the two vowels came to be pronounced alike, though there are dialects (e.g., in Ulster) where the distinction is maintained. The initial consonants in words such as *gnaw*, *know*, and *write* were pronounced until the 16th century. The spelling *gh* in words such as *light* and *night* indicates a consonant that has not been pronounced in most varieties of English since the 15th century but can still be heard in the speech of some Scots.

In situations where there is concern about the ability of individuals to interpret written forms there may be a recourse to iconic symbols as in this chart used by an American hospital for the patient to indicate degree of pain felt (Figure 7.3).

The use of symbols may partly have been motivated by the fact that patients at this hospital might speak a language other than English.

## Orthography and nationalism

The conservatism of the orthography conceals the kinds of changes that have taken place in pronunciation. Only in relic dialect areas is there any contemporary evidence of the earlier sounds. Most dialects do not have a recognized orthography and this creates problems for those who wish to raise the profile of the dialect. This situation has arisen in Ulster and in Scotland. The new power-sharing arrangements in Ulster led to a demand from the Republicans for Gaelic to be recognized as an official language to counter the prestige of English in government publications. This demand was met with a counter-demand from the Protestants to have Ulster Scots recognized as an official language also. Both demands were granted and this created a problem for the legislators because there was no agreed standardized form of Ulster Scots with a recognized orthography. Some of the early efforts to remedy this situation were met with ridicule and derision, but the legislation has not been repealed.

There is no agreed definition that distinguishes a dialect from a language. It used to be said that a language is a dialect with an army and a navy. This reflects the political importance of language. One of the first tasks of a new nation is to establish an official language for all government and bureaucratic business. When the Irish Republic became independent of the United Kingdom, it established Gaelic as the official language and required all officials to be able speak the language. Children were also instructed in the language from an early age. In Israel, Modern Hebrew had to be developed from Biblical Hebrew. After Norway became independent from Denmark, there was strong pressure to adopt a form of the language that was distinct from the Danish that had been used before independence. In Haiti there is disagreement about how Haitian Creole should be written. Since many Haitian Creole words are developed from French, they can be represented as such in their normal French orthographic forms. This makes it easier for those who speak French to recognize them. But this makes difficulties for those who do not speak French because the actual pronunciation of the words does not suggest the French written form. The choice is between a system based on the historical relation of Haitian Creole to French or one that is closer phonetically to the way people speak. Such a choice obviously has important political consequences. In the United States, Noah Webster set out to distance American English from British English by spelling changes, some of which have survived, such as the omission of the letter *u* in words such as *color*, still spelled *colour* in Britain, and spellings such as *theater* for British *theatre*, but many of his other innovations have not survived.

The national orthography, however, is maintained not by military force but by the educational system and the influential public media. There are a number of consequences of this. One is that there is a sense of "correctness" that is sustained by the written form. This provides the basis for a condemnation of nonstandard varieties, as was demonstrated by the furore aroused by the decision of the Oakland school board to promote Ebonics (see Chapter 5). There is also a belief that spelling errors reflect inadequate thought or knowledge. Thorstein Veblen pointed out the association of correctness with an elitist education. Spelling errors have become less prevalent recently with the influence of spell-checkers in word processing programs, but careful readers of the press will have noted that spell-checkers are not very good proof readers, since they will accept *that, than* or *then* without prejudice, although only one will be appropriate.

## The role of dictionaries

The codification of language in grammar books and dictionaries using the standard orthography gives the written form of language an authority that is denied to the spoken language. When new editions of dictionaries are published that include new words and expressions in current use, there is regularly a public protest about the lowering of standards and the inclusion of "colloquialisms." The label **colloquial** in a dictionary is a good example of the bias in favor of the written language. It suggests that there is something not quite legitimate or respectable about the word or expression. In fact, it simply means that the item is unlikely to be found in expository prose, but the implication of inferiority remains. The label **slang** is even more pejorative and refers to expressions that are not yet used by the majority of (educated) people, though that situation may change. (Words such as *coax, flimsy, fun, mob, sham,* and *snob* were once considered to be slang.)

Notions of "correct" grammar are also taken over from the written language. As was illustrated in Chapter 4, transcripts of speech show a very different kind of organization. It has frequently been pointed out that formal linguists in the Chomsky camp depend upon intuitions of grammaticality that are based on the written language, not on speech. (In fact, most people have little notion of how they actually speak, as can often be observed by their shocked reaction when they hear a recording of their informal conversation.) The "written bias in linguistics," as it has been called, has had unfortunate effects on the study of language.

## Spoken vs. written language

As was shown in Chapter 3, studies of children's language development by generativists have taken it for granted that children were trying to acquire the kind of linguistic knowledge that adults have, but young children do not have access to the kinds of written examples that the adults do. The written bias in linguistics places the emphasis on grammatical sentences, but sentences are not well-defined in the spoken language. (Charles Fries collected 200 definitions of sentence in his work investigating language use.) Speakers do not communicate mainly in forms that would count as grammatical sentences in writing. This is because everyday spoken interaction is dialogic, not a series of alternating monologues. As was pointed out in Chapter 4, meanings are a product of the combined efforts of speaker and hearer. Even the functionalists often treat language as monologic, paying less attention to the interactional context.

There are several essential differences between spoken language and written language. Spoken language is always localized in time and space. An utterance must have been made at a specific time and in a particular place, by a specific speaker, and it does not persist beyond the moment of delivery (except for speech recorded by electronic means). All deictic features (e.g., *I, you, here, this, tomorrow*, and so on) take their orientation from the speaker. Written texts are generally not closely identified with the time and place of production, though there are exceptions in the case of personal letters and legal documents.

Speech is dynamic, proceeds continuously, and is subject to monitoring and analysis by the speaker and hearer. If you miss something, you cannot go back to find out what that was. Written texts are static and durable. If you did not grasp something, you can go back and read it again.

Speech consists of a series of continuous movements, while written texts are composed of discrete items (e.g., letters, words, sentences) and the boundaries are usually fairly clear. Speech regularly occurs in situations where the speaker and hearer can see each other and can judge from visual clues as well as other indications whether what has been said was understood. Written texts (like this volume) are frequently produced without a specific reader in mind, though there is usually a type of reader envisaged. There is, however, no immediate feedback, so the writer has to guard against miscommunication by trying to avoid ambiguity or anything else that might mislead the reader.

Prosodic features (intonation and Stress) and paralinguistic features (such as fillers of the *um* and *er* type, speed, loudness, and emotional voice quality) play a very important role in spoken language, as do discourse markers (e.g., *oh, well, you know, I mean,* and so on) (see Chapter 4). In written language, punctuation and other devices, such as italics can give only a very crude indication of such features. Other indications have to be stated explicitly. This makes a very different style of communication.

One of the problems with the written bias in linguistics (when analyzing sentences out of context) is that writing does not represent some of the most important aspects of speech, namely intonation, speed, volume, and emphasis. As pointed out above, these are important features that are vital for the hearer in interpreting what is meant. A transcription of the words uttered will report what has been said but not how it is to be understood. It is not surprising that few theoretical linguists have paid much attention to intonation, though this is probably the first feature of verbal communication that infants pay attention to.

In sociolinguistic investigations, I have found that many speakers often include quoted dialogue in their narratives (see Chapter 4). The advantage of this method is that the narrator can indicate through mimicry the tone with which the remark was uttered.

The following is part of a story I was told by a woman in Ayr whose mother had arranged for her to start work in a carpet factory at the age of 16. She is explaining to her mother, who also works in the factory, why she wants to quit.

And I says to her "I'm no going back in there"
She says "How are you no going back in?"

I says "I'm no going back in
You should hear the swears of them in there"
She says "They don't swear in the finishing room"
I says "Do they no?
You want to come and hear them"
So there was a big Italian woman worked with her
And Ina Solotti says to her "Who said the feenishing room didnae
swear Mary?"
My mother says "Me"
"Well" she says "we've nothing on them
Away you go and listen to them at their door" she says
"and you'll get the shock of your life"

The use of quoted dialogue avoids the necessity of saying explicitly what the original speaker's attitude was, and the hearer can draw his or her own conclusions. In written work, novelists are forced to employ adverbs to indicate the manner of speaking as in *he said angrily, she whispered softly,* or descriptive verbs as in *he growled, she pleaded.* In Scotland, as reported in Chapter 5, I found that working-class speakers were less likely to use descriptive adverbs such as *softly* and *angrily* than the middle-class speakers. I interpreted this difference as a reluctance on the part of the working-class speakers to impose their views on the hearer, in contrast to the middle-class speakers, who were often quite emphatic in expressing their opinions. The use of quoted dialogue as in the above story allows the person hearing it to interpret the attitude and intention of the participants from the way they speak.

## The transcription of speech

Interest in the ways in which language is used in communication (Chapter 4) has led to different approaches to the representation of spoken language in writing. It may seem paradoxical that most analysis of talk-in-action is carried out through transcripts of tape-recorded speech, but this is necessary for a number of reasons. Being able to study the transcript at a slower speed than the rate of articulated speech allows the analyst to look for patterns and relationships in the discourse. It is easier to keep track of what is happening in a conversation when it has been carefully transcribed.

The frequency with which words or expressions are used can be easily determined from a computerized concordance listing all the words that a speaker has used.

Different models of transcription have been used. There was a famous example of an attempt to provide an exhaustive transcription of part of an interview. The transcript was made in phonetic transcription and included much prosodic and paralinguistic information. The authors report that it took 25–30 hours to transcribe the five minute extract. The result was a text that was difficult to read and contained much information that was redundant to any understanding of the interaction. Nobody has attempted to replicate this experiment. Many Conversation Analysts (Chapter 4) who provide transcripts of actual speech have employed spellings, such as *gunnuh, wuz, yer, jus,* and *yihknow* in the attempt to suggest the sound of the words. This is known as **eye-dialect** and is similar to the use of variant spellings by fiction writers who try to indicate nonstandard speech. There are at least two problems with this approach. One is that it tends to suggest a rather negative (or at least patronizing) attitude toward the speakers. The other is that some of these spellings are simply a clumsy way of indicating the kinds of vowel reduction that occurs in the speech of standard speakers but are not normally shown in writing. A third problem is that it is often unclear what actual phonetic quality the nonstandard spelling is intended to represent. There are obviously advantages in being able to indicate some dialect pronunciations and expressions but they have to be in a form that the reader can interpret. In the example above, *no* (= *not*), *feenishing,* and *didnae* (= *didn't*) are all indications of the Scottish speakers, but they should cause no problems for most readers.

Another problem in transcribing speech is how to divide up larger sequences. Few transcribers will attempt to represent speech as a succession of sentences, since the sentence is not well defined in speech. Some analysts employ the notion of an **intonation unit**, usually a sequence of from one to at most seven words. These units reflect the "chunking" that makes impromptu speech usually much easier to follow than a written text read out as a lecture. Transcripts of this kind, however, tend require a great deal of space and thus may not be suitable for lengthy extracts. Other analysts represent connected speech in lines that roughly correspond to the notion of a clause (as in the above example), and this method has a familiar appearance (like that of a Shakespeare play). Some analysts of conversations with several speakers have employed a transcription modeled on musical notation, showing each speaker on a separate line. This method is helpful for displaying the interaction among the speakers.

Most transcripts of speech do not employ many punctuation marks. Some analysts use a period to indicate falling intonation, as at the end of a sequence, and comma to indicate that the speaker is pausing but intends to continue. A question mark is often used to indicate rising indication at the end of a section. Some (but not all) transcribers use quotation marks to indicate quoted dialogue. The problem with this use of punctuation is that it differs from its use in writing. Punctuation in writing is a way of segmenting units in a meaningful way that serves some of the function of intonation in speech, but it is a very different system. For example, the question mark always signals a question in writing, but not all spoken questions end with rising intonation. Also, rising intonation at the end of a sequence does not always indicate a question. Commas are also used much more frequently in writing and for a variety of different purposes. There is no obvious function for a semi-colon in transcribing speech.

## Literacy

Literacy is far from universal. Many societies have survived without it, and until recently only a minority of the population of any society could read and write. In fact, even the notion of a language as a distinct entity may not exist in communities that do not employ writing. Anthropologists have found that many small-scale societies do not even have a name for their own language. Until a language is written down there is less need for a label to distinguish it from other forms of speech, but once it is written down it takes on a distinct character. We use words such as English, French, and Russian as if they were well-defined entities, but many linguists believe that the notion of a national language cannot be clearly specified in any useful, technical sense.

Writing makes possible many activities that would be difficult if not impossible otherwise. The most obvious example is science. There is no illiterate science. No matter how many experiments are carried out, the results do not become part of scientific knowledge until they are written down. It is not necessary to publish these results but unless they are recorded somewhere, they cannot be included as a contribution to scientific discovery. Writing is also employed for artistic purposes. Here it is less essential. There are many forms of oral art (it seems paradoxical to call them oral literature) and we know from works such as the *Iliad* and *Beowulf* that highly sophisticated poetry can be created without recourse to writing. The fact that we know about them now, of course, is because at some date they were written down, though that was not the case when they were composed. It is undeniable, however, that most of what we consider literature was created in written form. Even the works of Shakespeare, which were performed in oral form, were written down at some point, though whether completely before stage performance or after remains unclear. The existence of written literature from Old English times to the present day allows us to learn about people and situations that we could not have experienced directly. Nor could we have known enough people to tell us about such things orally. We have to be deeply grateful to those Sumerians who began to record language in written symbols and to all those who contributed to the writing system that we take for granted now. It is almost (but not quite) as important a development as the evolution of language itself.

## SUGGESTIONS FOR FURTHER READING

A good account of the development of writing can be found in Florian Coulmas *The Writing Systems of the World*. The best book on writing systems is Peter Daniels and William Bright's *The World's Writing Systems* though I.J. Gelb's *A Study of Writing* is much easier to consult. The impact of literacy on society is examined by Walter Ong in *Orality and Literacy* and by Jack Goody in *The Interface between the Written and the Oral*. A different perspective is presented by Ivan Illich and Barry Sanders in *ABC: The Alphabetization of the Popular Mind*. The ways in which language standards are established and maintained are examined by Deborah Cameron in *Verbal Hygiene*. David R. Olson *The World on Paper* explains many of the characteristics of reading and writing. Per Linell's *The Written Bias in Linguistics* makes a strong case against the methodology of the generativists, particularly Chomsky. Wallace Chafe's *Discourse, Consciousness, and Time* examines the differences between speaking and writing. *Spontaneous Spoken Language* by Jim Miller and Regina Weinert shows how the syntax of spoken language differs from that of written language. Angus McIntosh, Michael Samuels, and Michael Benskin produced the *Linguistic Atlas of Late Mediaeval English.*

# Afterword

The psychologist George Miller once wrote an article with the title 'The magic number seven, plus or minus two.' There are of course many more than seven ways of looking at language, but seven has a special significance in European folklore and George Miller also pointed out its relevance to social science. There is, however, no reason for the reader interested in language to ignore many other ways of looking at language. There are books dealing with language in many sections of the library other than those classified as language or linguistics and there is plenty to interest the inquisitive reader. Here are some areas to explore.

## Phonology

As I stated earlier, I decided to omit examination of phonology from Chapter 3 on form, but that does not mean that phonology is unimportant or uninteresting. Phonetics deals with sounds in universal terms. Phonology deals with the use of those sounds in a particular language. One of the original insights of 20th-century linguistics was the recognition of the phoneme as a significant unit of linguistic form. The history of the study of phonology in the past eighty years is almost as complex as that of syntax, and the disagreements have been equally strong. Reading about phonology is not for the faint-hearted but the reward is finding out about the very complex ways in which some languages organize their sound systems.

## Morphology

I also excluded morphology, for similar reasons, though in some ways it is an easier topic to explore. The study of morphology includes the grammatical inflections, such as those that in English indicate tense or number, but it also examines the process of word-formation. This is a topic that is of interest from both a contemporary and a historical perspective. From the contemporary perspective, it is relevant to how language is stored in the brain. From a historical perspective, understanding how words evolved can shed light on past society, for example, knowing that the contemporary word *lord* developed from an Old English compound meaning "keeper of the bread" and *lady* from another Old English compound meaning "maker of the bread."

## Evolution of language

For more than a hundred years after the Société de Linguistique in Paris in 1866 banned the publication of any more articles on the origin of language, the topic of language evolution was essentially a taboo subject. It was believed that there was no credible evidence that could help to resolve the question of how human beings came to use language, so any discussion of the subject would be mere speculation. Recent work in archeology, animal communication, genetics, and brain research has provided a vast array of information that is relevant to theorizing about how language could have evolved. This is now one of the hottest topics in the field of language.

## Language development

Chomsky's claims about the innate language ability of humans, paradoxically, initiated a flood of research into how children's language develops. Although a great deal has been discovered through all this activity, much remains in dispute and this is a lively field to explore. As with study of syntax, there is a sharp division between the Chomskyans and the functionalists, but there is much to be gained from the work of both approaches.

## Bilingualism and second language learning

The migration of people from one country to another often results in the need to learn a new language. This situation has stimulated both research and commerce. Teaching English as a Second Language has become a major industry providing employment for a variety of native speakers. At the same time, there has been much research carried out to determine both the best ways to teach a second language and also the cognitive consequences of knowing more than one language. This latter aspect is particularly significant for schools dealing with immigrant children whose knowledge of English is limited. There are also complicated political factors that affect efforts to provide bilingual education.

## Pidgins and Creoles

In many colonial situations the result of contact between speakers who did not share a common language was the development of a compromise form of communication that was not anyone's primary language. Such languages, called pidgin languages, developed in many parts of the world. When children in such places began using this language as their primary form of communication, the pidgin evolved into what is called a creole language. Such languages can become the dominant language in a community as has happened in Papua New Guinea and in Haiti, for example.

## Language disorders

For over a hundred years there has been interest in the effect of traumatic injuries to the brain that can affect language. For a long time, this research was hampered by the fact that precise information about the damage done by the injury could be obtained only by postmortem investigation. New methods of studying the brain, such as functional magnetic resonance imagery, now provide much information on patients who are still alive. This has led to many hypotheses about language functioning but as is generally the case with linguistic matters more is in dispute than generally accepted. It is, however, another very hot topic in linguistics at the present.

## Onomastics

Onomastics is study of names and has two main branches. One is the investigation of the origin of names, both of people and of places. In the latter case, identifying the source of a place-name can often be helpful for understanding the earlier history of a region for which there are no written records. In the case of people, naming traditions differ across the world and may reflect aspects of social organization. For example, some societies employ a practice of patronymics whereby a child is named after an ancestor. My own name, Macaulay, reflects the Gaelic practice of naming after the father, where *Mac* is "the son of" and *Aulay* would have been my father's name, but this is a relic of an older system. My own son is not MacRonald. (I was also slightly disturbed to find out recently that the Scandinavian root of *Aulay* means "relic of the gods" and I am not sure how to react to this piece of information.)

## Literature

It may seem redundant to say it, but literary works can be studied by the methods of linguistics. For example, the topic of metrics in poetry is one that can be explored using the methods of phonetics and phonology. The identification of authorship in cases of dubious attribution can be investigated by the use of quantified methods, as has happened with regard to Shakespeare's works.

\* \* \*

I have been making use of libraries for more than sixty years and yet I still experience a feeling of excitement when I am able to browse the shelves in search of a book on some topic that interests me at that time. Often, I come across works I did not know about that turn out to be more useful than the one I had come to find. A library is still a treasure-house of knowledge, though the internet is now taking over some of its functions. Both the library and the internet will be more rewarding if you know what you are looking for. I hope the previous chapters will have roused your curiosity enough to explore some of the topics discussed in them and lead to greater understanding.

## SUGGESTIONS FOR FURTHER READING

A very readable introduction to phonology is David Odden's *Introducing Phonology*. An older work that is still relevant is Roger Lass's

*Phonology.* Stephen Anderson's *Phonology in the Twentieth Century* is helpful but the field has changed so much since then that the 20th century seems like the distant past. Those who are feeling particularly brave and want to find out about a more recent approach to phonology might venture a look in Diana Archangeli and Terence Langendoen's *Optimality Theory* and René Kager's *Optimality Theory*, but they should be prepared to be totally baffled.

The best introduction to morphology is Peter Matthew's *Morphology*. Another readable work is Laurie Bauer's *Introducing Linguistic Morphology*. Bauer's *English Word-formation* and Hans Marchand's *The Categories and Types of Present-day English Word-Formation* provide much information about the morphology of English. Andrew Spencer provides an example of a more recent approach in *An Introduction to Word Structure in Generative Grammar*.

The field of language evolution is a fast-moving target. Christine Kenneally's *The First Word* is a very readable summary of recent approaches to the topic. Derek Bickerton has written extensively on the evolution of language. He writes very clearly and makes his points very forcefully. His latest work is *Adam's Tongue* (though he may have three more books out on the topic by the time this work appears). Robin Dunbar's *Grooming, Gossip, and the Evolution of Language* takes an original view of the situation and is very easy to read. James R. Hurford's *The Origins of Meaning* is a comprehensive account of the topic.

*The Development of Language* by Jean Berko Gleason provides a very readable view of children's language development. Slightly more challenging is Eve Clark's *First Language Acquisition*. A plausible account of children's language development can be seen in Michael Tomasello's *Constructing a Language* and in the articles the volume entitled *Beyond Nature-nurture*, edited by Michael Tomasello and Dan Slobin.

Dennis Preston's *Sociolinguistics and Second Language Learning* is a good introduction to the topic of second language learning. Suzanne Romaine's *Bilngualism* covers that topic fully in a very readable account. Rod Ellis's massive *The Study of Second Language Acquisition* provides a wide survey of the field.

Suzanne Romaine's *Pidgin and Creole Languages* is the best short introduction to the topic. John Holm's *Introduction to Pidgin and Creoles* is also quite accessible. Salikoko Mufwene's *The Ecology of Language Evolution* discusses the role of pidgins and creoles in language change. R.B. Le Page and Andrée Tabouret-Keller's *Acts of Identity* examines the role of a creole language in a community. The most entertaining and readable work on this topic is Derek Bickerton's narrative account of his work as a creolist, *Bastard Tongues*. If you have time for only one book, this is the one to choose.

The study of language and the brain is another trendy subject and remark-able discoveries are frequently reported in the popular press, but often the claims are premature and contradicted by later studies. The best introduction is Lorraine Obler and Kris Gjerlow's *Language and the Brain*. David Caplan's *Language Structure, Processing and Disorders* provides more detailed information. Philip Lieberman's *Toward an Evolutionary Biology of Language* contains information on more recent brain research. For more detailed information, consult Brigitte Stemmer and Harry Whitaker's *Handbook of Neurolinguistics* and Yosef Grodzinsky and Katrin Amunts' *Broca's Region*, but be warned: these are not easy bedtime reading.

For place-names, the most readable account is Kenneth Cameron's *English Place-Names*. Adrian Room's *Dictionary of Place-Names in the British Isles* is also easy to consult as is C.M.Matthews' *Place-names of the English-speaking World*. The major work is Eilert Ekwall's *The Concise Oxford Dictionary of English Place-Names*, now in its fourth edition. For Scottish place-names, consult W.F.H.Nicolaisen's *Scottish Place-Names*. For surnames, consult P.H.Reaney's *The Origin of English Surnames* and his *Dictionary of British Surnames*. Elsdon Smith provides information on *American Surnames*.

About forty years ago there was a flood of works looking at literature from the perspective of linguistics but it now seems more like a trickle. Geoffrey Leech's *A Linguistic Guide to English Poetry* and Jonathan Culler's *Structural Poetics* remain two of the best examples and Donald Freeman's edited volume *Linguistics and Literary Style* contains a use-ful selection of articles. For an example of the application of structur-alism to poetry, see the analysis of a poem by W.B.Yeats in Roman Jakobson' s *Verbal Art, Verbal Sign, Verbal Time*. You'll be amazed by the complexity of the analysis and how little illumination it sheds on the poem. The best recent contribution to the linguistic analysis of literature is Nigel Fabb's *Language and Literary Structure*, though it is not easy reading. An even more technical approach to poetry is Nigel Fabb and Morris Halle's *Metre in Poetry*.

# Glossary

[The glosses are not intended as complete definitions but simply to indicate as briefly as possible how the words are used in linguistic descriptions]

**acoustic analysis** The use of spectrographic analysis of sound frequencies to identify differences in pronunciation

**active voice** The syntactic form where the subject is typically the actor or cause of the action, in contrast to the Passive Voice.

**adverbial phrase** A syntactic group that functions as an adverb

**African American Vernacular English (AAVE)** The form of speech used by many African-Americans as their informal style

**affricate** A consonant that combines the closure of a stop consonant with a slow release resembling a fricative

**adjacency pairs** A feature of ordinary conversation where one utterance carries the expectation of a response, e.g., a greeting or a question

**algorithmic model** A procedure for applying a set of rules in a mechanical fashion

**alveolar consonants** Consonants produced by contact between the tongue and the alveolar ridge behind the teeth

**alphabetic writing system** A system of writing in which the characters represent individual sounds

**analogy** A process in linguistic change in which a form is changed by comparison with another

**analytic proposition** A statement whose truth or falsity is determined solely by the meaning of the words

**apocope** The loss of the last syllable or sound of a word

**apparent-time studies** Sociolinguistic investigations which extrapolate linguistic changes from differences in the speech of younger and older people

**aspirated consonant** A stop consonant that is released quickly with a following short burst of noise

**assimilation** The change through which two sounds come to be articulated in a more similar way

**bleaching** A semantic change which leads to the loss of meaning

**case** A term used in some grammatical descriptions to indicate syntactic relations, such as Agent or Location

**case grammar** A syntactic model based on case structure

**chain shift** A situation where a change in one sound has a direct effect on another sound

**cliché** A trite expression

**click sounds** Stop consonants produced with an airstream caused by a closure in the back of the mouth

**colloquial** Dictionary term for the kind of language used in everyday speech but implying that it is nonstandard

**communities of practice** A term used in sociolinguistics to refer to groups of people who meet regularly

**comparative method** A way of analyzing older languages in terms of words with similar meanings to determine origins and relationships

**constituent structure** The grouping of words into units that are necessary for syntactic analysis

**construction grammar** A form of syntactic analysis that includes basic units larger than single words

**content words** Words that refer to aspects of reality

**conversation analysis** The systematic analysis of how people use language in everyday situations

**cuneiform** The wedge-shaped characters used in many early writing systems

**deep structure** The level of syntactic analysis postulated in early versions of transformational grammar that contained all the necessary semantic information

**deictic terms** Words that take part of their meaning from the speaker

**definite article** The form *the* used to indicate reference to a particular situation

**discourse markers** Words used by speakers that convey attitudes but do not otherwise affect the basic meaning of the utterance

**Ebonics** A term sometimes used to refer to African American Vernacular English, but not accepted by most linguists

**ejectives** Stop consonants produced with a closed glottis that sound like a heavily aspirated stop

**E-language** The term used by Noam Chomsky to refer to the actual use of language

**embedded** An embedded structure is one contained within another

**entailment** The meaning that necessarily follows from any assertion

**epenthesis** A change that involves the insertion of a sound in a word

**eye-dialect** A way of representing nonstandard speech to suggest how it sounds

**fricatives** Consonants produced by the approximation of two articulators without actual contact

**function words**The small grammatical words that do not have any direct reference to the physical world

**functional grammar** A form of syntactic analysis that takes context into consideration

**generalized conversational implicature** The kind of inference that listeners are likely to draw from an utterance, although it is not explicitly stated

**generic** A term used to refer to a whole category rather than a specific instance

**glottal stop** A consonant formed by complete closure of the vocal cords

**glottis** The location of the vocal cords

**grammaticalization** The process by which a content word changes its function and meaning to become a function word

**Great Vowel Shift** The term used to refer to a chain shift of English vowels in the 16th century

**homographs** Words that are spelled the same way but are pronounced differently

**homophones** Words that sound the same but have distinct meanings

**I-language** The term used by Noam Chomsky to refer to a speaker's linguistic competence

**idiom** A term used to refer to a sequence of words with a meaning different from their literal interpretation

**illocutionary act** A term used in the description of the communicative function of an utterance

**immediate constituent analysis** A form of analysis that groups words into syntactic units

**implicature** The inference contained in an utterance

**implosive** A consonant produced by sucking in air with the vocal cords tightly closed

**indefinite article** The article *a(n)* used with singular nouns in English

**International Phonetic Alphabet (IPA)** The system developed for the transcription all possible sounds in any human language

**interrogative** An utterance that asks a question

**intonation** The rise and fall of the pitch of the voice

**intonation unit** A part of an utterance that has its own intonation pattern

**kernel sentence** The term used by Noam Chomsky to refer to the basic form of sentences in a transformational grammar

**labial consonants** Consonants produced with the lips

**laterals** Consonants where the airstream passes on one side of the tongue

**lenition** A change in which the articulation of a sound weakens, e.g., from a stop to a fricative

**lexical item** The term used to refer to a unit of vocabulary

**lexical tone** The use of pitch level to distinguish words that differ in meaning

**linguistic competence** The term used by Noam Chomsky to refer to the speaker's knowledge of a language

**linguistic intuition** The term used to refer to a speaker's ability to decide whether a given form is grammatical or not

**linguistic performance** The term used by Noam Chomsky to refer to a speaker's use of a language

**linguistic variable** A sociolinguistic term for a linguistic set of forms that is used differently by members of a speech community

**linguistic variant** One of the instances of a linguistic variable

**locutionary act** The production of an utterance

**Logical Form (LF)** The term used by Noam Chomsky in his later work to refer to the meaning of a sentence

**logographic writing system** A writing system in which the symbols stand for whole words

**metathesis** A change that involves the reversal of the order of two sounds

**Middle English** The term used to refer to the period in the history of the English language from the 11th century to the end of the fourteenth

**minimal responses** Conversational ways of acknowledging to a speaker that you are paying attention to what is being said

**Minimalist Program** The latest syntactic model proposed by Noam Chomsky

**morphology** The study of the forms of words

**nasals** Consonant sounds produced by letting the airstream pass through the nose

**Neogrammarian Hypothesis** The claim made by some 19th-century German grammarians that sound changes occurred without exception

**new information** The term used to refer to the introduction of a topic into a conversation

**non-rhotic varieties** A term used to refer to those dialects of English in which the sound /r/ is not pronounced before consonants or at the end of words

**noun phrase (NP)** The term used to refer to a syntactic structure that contains a noun

**Old English** The term used to refer to the language spoken in England in the period 500–1100.

**old information** The term used to refer to topics that have earlier been introduced into the conversation

**palatography** A technique used in phonetics to determine the place of articulation of some stop consonants

**paralinguistic features** Features of speaking such as speech rate, loudness, or hoarseness that are not part of a linguistic analysis

**parameters** A term used by Noam Chomsky to refer to non-universal features of language that are found in individual languages

**parole** The term used by Ferdinand de Saussure to refer to the use of language

**particularized conversational implicature** A term used to refer to inferences that a listener may make in a specific situation although they are not explicitly stated

**passive voice** A construction in which the subject of the verb is the recipient of the action

**performatives** Utterances such as promising, betting or swearing an oath which perform the function in doing so

**phoneme** The term used to refer to the basic unit of sound in a language system

**Phonetic Form (PF)** The term used by Noam Chomsky in his later work to refer to what he had previously called surface structure

**phonological component** The part of a language description that deals with how sounds are used systematically

**phonology** The study of the systematic use of sounds in a language

**phrasal verb** A verb that consists of more than one word, e.g., *put out*

**Phrase Structure Grammar (PSG)** The term used to refer to the form of grammar that does not involve transformational rules

**phrase structure rules** The rules for identifying the constituents in a syntactic structure

**phrase structure tree** A graphic display of the constituents identified by the Phrase Structure Rules

**pitch** The acoustic frequency produced by the vibration of the vocal cords

**polysemy** The term used to refer to the range of meanings that a word may have

**pragmatics** The study of the use of utterances in context

**presupposition** What can be assumed to be true from an utterance even though it is not openly stated

**prosodic features** Those aspects of speech, such as intonation and stress, that are part of any utterance but are not usually included in grammatical analyses

**Proto-Indo-European (PIE)** The hypothetical ancestor of most European languages that has been reconstructed by means of the comparative method

**real-time studies** Sociolinguistic investigations of linguistic change that are based on samples of speech from different periods

**Received Pronunciation (RP)** The term used to refer to the prestige accent in England

**Relevance theory** A pragmatic theory that argues for the importance of context on understanding what has been said

**rhotic varieties** A term used to refer to those dialects of English in which the sound /r/ is pronounced before consonants and at the end of words

**rounded vowels** Vowels which are articulated with rounded lips

**scriptoria** Medieval centers of manuscript production

**semantic component** The part of a generative grammar that deals with meaning

**semantics** The study of meaning

**sentence** The basic unit for formal approaches to syntactic analysis

**shifters** Words that take their reference from the speaker, e.g., *I, here*

**speech accommodation** The term used to refer to the ways in which speakers may adjust to interlocutors of different status

**Speech Act Theory** The name given to the study of the function of utterances in interpersonal communication

**signified** The term used by Ferdinand de Saussure for the meaning of an expression

**signifier** The term used by Ferdinand de Saussure for the form of an expression

**social networks** A term used in sociolinguistics to refer to the groups with which a speaker regularly interacts

**sound-image** The term used by Ferdinand de Saussure for the phonetic form of an expression

**Standard English** The term used to refer to the non-regional form of English that is used in national media and government communications

**stop consonants** Consonants that are produced with a complete closure in the vocal tract and released suddenly

**stress** The term used to refer to the degree of emphasis on a syllable

**surface structure** The term used in early generative grammars to refer to the output of the transformational rules

**syllabic writing systems** Writing systems in which the characters refer to syllables rather than to individual sounds

**syncope** A form of linguistic change that consists of the loss of a syllable in the middle of a word

**synthetic** A term used (in contrast to *analytic*) for a statement that can only be verified by reference to the situation

**theta-marking** A term used in later generative grammars to indicate syntactic roles such as Agent or Instrument

**Transformational Grammar (TG)** The form of syntactic analysis proposed by Noam Chomsky which employs rules to transform underlying (deep)structures to their surface form

**trills** Consonant sounds produced by the rapid movement of the tongue

**turn-taking rules** A description of the ways in which conversationalists take turns in speaking

**unaspirated consonant** A stop consonant that (in contrast to an aspirated consonant) is not followed immediately a short burst of noise

**Universal Grammar (UG)** The term used by Noam Chomsky to refer to the innate ability human beings have to develop language

**uniformitarian principle** The hypothesis that the kind of processes that affect linguistic change are no different now from what they were in the past

**unrounded vowels** Vowels that are produced with no rounding of the lips

**utterance** The term used to refer to a spoken group of words

**velar consonants** Consonants that are produced through contact between the back of the tongue and the velum

**velum** The soft palate

**verb phrase (VP)** A syntactic constituent in which the most important word is the verb

**vocal cords** A pair of bands or folds in the larynx that vibrate in the production of voiced sounds

**voiced sounds** Sounds that are produced with the vocal cords vibrating

**voiceless sounds** Sounds that are produced with no vibration of the vocal cords

**voice onset time (VOT)** The point at which the vocal cords begin vibrating after the release of a stop consonant

# References

Abercrombie, David. 1967. *Elements of General Phonetics*. Edinburgh: Edinburgh University Press.

Anderson, Stephen. 1985. *Phonology in the Twentieth Century*. Chicago: University of Chicago Press.

Archangeli, Diana and D. Terence Langendoen (eds.) 1997. *Optimality Theory: An Overview*. Oxford: Blackwell.

Austin, John L. 1962. *How to Do Things with Words*. London: Oxford University Press.

Barfield, Owen. 1954. *History in English Words,* New ed. London: Faber and Faber.

Bauer, Laurie. 1983. *English Word-formation*. Cambridge: Cambridge University Press.

—— 2003. *Introducing Linguistic Morphology*. Edinburgh: Edinburgh University Press.

Bellwood, Peter and Colin Renfrew (eds.) 2002. *Examining the Farming/language Dispersal Hypothesis*. Cambridge: McDonald Institute for Archaeological Research.

Bickerton, Derek. 2008. *Bastard Tongues: A Trailblazing Linguist Finds Clues to Our Common Humanity in the World's Lowliest Languages*. New York: Hill and Wang.

—— 2009. *Adam's Tongue: How Humans Made Language, How Language made Humans*. New York: Hill and Wang.

Blake, N.F. 1996. *A History of the English Language*. New York: New York University Press.

Bloomfield, Leonard. 1926. A set of postulates for the science of language. *Language* 2: 153–164.

Blum-Kulka, Shoshana. 1997. *Dinner Talk: Cultural Patterns of Sociability and Socialization in Family Discourse*. Mahwah, NJ: Lawrence Erlbaum.

Boeckx, Cedric. 2010. *Language in Cognition: Uncovering Mental Structures and the Rules behind them*. Chichester: Wiley-Blackwell.

Boye, Kasper and Elisabeth Engberg-Pedersen (eds.) 2010. *Language Usage and Language Structure*. Berlin: De Gruyter Mouton.

Brinton, Laurel J. and Elizabeth Closs Traugott. 2005. *Lexicalization and Language Change*. Cambridge: Cambridge University Press.

Bronstein, Arthur J. 1960. *The Pronunciation of American English: A Introduction to Phonetics*. New York: Appleton-Century-Crofts.

Cameron, Kenneth. 1961. *English Place-Names*. London: Batsford.

Caplan, David. 1992. *Language Structure, Processing and Disorders*. Cambridge, Mass.: MIT Press.

Cassidy, Frederick G. (ed.) 1985–2002. *Dictionary of American Regional English*. Cambridge, Mass.: Belknap Press.

Chafe, Wallace. 1994. *Discourse, Consciousness, and Time: The Flow and Displacement of Conscious Experience in Speaking and Writing*. Chicago: University of Chicago Press.

Chambers, J.K. 1995. *Sociolinguistic Theory*. Oxford: Blackwell.

Chambers, J.K., Peter Trudgill, and Natalie Schilling-Estes. 2002. *The Handbook of Language Variation and Change*. Oxford: Blackwell.

Chomsky, Noam. 1957. *Syntactic Structures*. The Hague: Mouton.

—— 1965. *Aspects of the Theory of Syntax*. Cambridge, Mass.: MIT Press.

Clark, Eve. V. 2003. *First Language Acquisition*. Cambridge: Cambridge University Press.

Coates, Jennifer. 1996. *Women Talk: Conversation between Women Friends*. Oxford: Blackwell.

—— 2003. *Men Talk: Stories in the Making of Masculinities*. Oxford: Blackwell.

Coulmas, Florian. 1989. *The Writing Systems of the World*. Oxford: Blackwell.

Coupland, Justine (ed.) 2000. *Small Talk*. London: Pearson Education.

Coupland, Nikolas. 1988. *Dialect in Use: Sociolinguistic Variation in Cardiff English*. Cardiff: University of Wales Press.

Croft, William and D.Alan Cruse. 2004. *Cognitive Linguistics*. Cambridge: Cambridge University Press.

Cruttenden, Alan. 1986. *Intonation*. Cambridge: Cambridge University Press.

—— 2008. *Gimson's Pronunciation of English*. London: Hodder Education.

Culicover, Peter W. 1999. *Syntactic Nuts: Hard Cases, Syntactic Theory, and Language Acquisition*. New York: Oxford University Press.

Culicover, Peter W. and Ray Jacendoff. 2005. *Simpler Syntax*. New York: Oxford University Press.

Culler, Jonathan. 1975. *Structuralist Poetics: Structuralism, Linguistics, and the Study of Literature*. London: Routledge and Kegan Paul.

Daniels, Peter D. and William Bright (eds.) 1996. *The World's Writing Systems*. New York: Oxford University Press.

Deacon, Terence W. 1997. *The Symbolic Species: The Co-evolution of Language and the Brain.* New York: W.W.Norton.

Devitt, Michael. 2006. *Ignorance of Language.* Oxford: Oxford University Press.

Downing, Pamela, Susan D. Lima, and Michael Noonan (eds.) 1992. *The Linguistics of Literacy.* Amsterdam: John Benjamins.

Downes, William. 1998. *Language and Society.* Cambridge: Cambridge University Press.

Dunbar, Robin. 1996. *Grooming, Gossip, and the Evolution of Language.* Cambridge, Mass.: Harvard University Press.

Eckert, Penelope. 2000. *Linguistic Variation as Social Practice: The Linguistic Construction of Identity in Belten High.* Oxford: Blackwell.

Eckert, Penelope and Sally McConnell-Ginet. 2003. *Language and Gender.* Cambridge: Cambridge University Press.

Eckert, Penelope and John R. Rickford (eds.) 2001. *Style and Sociolinguistic Variation.* Cambridge: Cambridge University Press.

Eggins, Suzanne and Diana Slade. 1997. *Analyzing Casual Conversation.* London: Cassell.

Ekwall. Eilert. 1960. *The Concise Oxford Dictionary of English Place-Names,* 4th ed. Oxford: Oxford University Press.

Ellis, Rod. 2008. *The Study of Second Language Acquisition,* 2nd ed. Oxford: Oxford University Press.

Ezcurdia, Maite, Robert J. Stainton, and Christopher Viger (eds.) 2004. *New Essays in the Philosophy of Language and Mind.* Calgary: University of Calgary Press.

Fabb, Nigel. 2002. *Language and Literary Structure: Linguistic Analysis of Form in Verse and Narrative.* Cambridge: Cambridge University Press.

Fabb, Nigel and Morris Halle. 2008. *Metre in Poetry: A New Theory.* Cambridge: Cambridge University Press.

Feagin, Crawford. 1979. *Variation and Change in Alabama English: A Sociolinguistic Study of the White Community.* Washington, DC: Georgetown University Press.

Fontanella de Weinberg, Maria. 1974. *Un Aspecto Sociolingüistico del Español Bonaerense: La –s in Bahia Blanca.* Bahia Blanca: Cuadernos de Lingüistica.

Fought, Carmen. 2003. *Chicano English in Context.* Basingstoke: Palgrave Macmillan.

—— 2006. *Language and Ethnicity.* Cambridge: Cambridge University Press.

Foulkes, Paul and Gerard Docherty (eds.) 1999. *Urban Voices: Accent Studies in the British Isles.* London: Arnold.

References 187

Freed, Alice F. and Susan Ehrlich (eds.). 2010. *"Why Do You Ask?" The Function of Questions in Institutional Discourse*. New York: Oxford University Press.

Freeman, Donald C. (ed.) 1970. *Linguistics and Literary Style*. New York: Holt, Rinehart and Winston.

Gelb, I.J. 1963. *A Study of Writing*. Chicago: University of Chicago Press.

Gimson, A.C. 1962. *An Introduction to the Pronunciation of English*. London: Edward Arnold.

Givón, T. 1995. *Functionalism and Grammar*. Amsterdam: John Benjamins.

Glauser, Beat. 1974. *The Scottish-English Linguistic Border: Lexical Aspects*. Bern: Francke Verlag.

Gleason, Jean Berko. 2005. *The Development of Language*, 6th ed. Boston: Pearson/Allyn and Bacon.

Goldberg, Adele E. 1995. *Constructions: A Construction Approach to Argument Structure*. Chicago: University of Chicago Press.

Grodzinsky, Yosef and Katrin Amunts (eds.) 2006. *Broca's Region*. Oxford : Oxford University Press.

Haiman, John. 1998. *Talk is Cheap: Sarcasm, Alienation, and the Evolution of Language*. New York: Oxford University Press.

Halliday, Michael A.K. 1973. *Explorations in the Functions of Language*. London: Edward Arnold.

Hartmann, Katharina. 2000. *Right Node Raising and Gapping: Interface Conditions on Prosodic Deletion*. Amsterdam: John Benjamins.

Holm, John A. 2000. *An Introduction to Pidgin and Creoles*. Cambridge: Cambridge University Press.

Holmes, Janet. 1992. *An Introduction to Sociolinguistics*. London: Longman.

—— 1995. *Women, Men and Politeness*. London: Longman.

Hopper, Robert. 1992. *Telephone Conversation*. Bloomington: Indiana University Press.

Huck, Geoffrey J. and John A. Goldsmith. 1995. *Ideology and Linguistic Theory: Noam Chomsky and the Deep Structure Debates*. London: Routledge.

Hurford, James R. 2007. *The Origins of Meaning*. New York: Oxford University Press.

Hymes, Dell H. 1974. *Foundations in Sociolinguistics: An Ethnographic Approach*. Philadelphia: University of Pennsylvania Press.

—— 2003. *Now I know only so far: Essays in Ethnopoetics*. Lincoln, Nebraska: University of Nebraska Press.

Illich, Ivan and Barry Sanders. 1988. *ABC: The Alphabetization of the Popular Mind*. New York: Random House.

Jackendoff, Ray. 2002. *Foundations of Language: Brain, Meaning, Grammar, Evolution.* New York: Oxford University Press.

Jakobson, Roman. 1985. *Verbal Art, Verbal Sign, Verbal Time,* ed. by Krystyna Pomarska and Stephen Rudy. Minneapolis: University of Minnesota Press.

Janicki, Karol. 2006. *Language Misconceived: Arguing for Applied Cognitive Linguistics.* Mahwah, NJ: Lawrence Erlbaum.

Jaworski, Adam. 1993. *The Power of Silence: Social and Pragmatic Perspectives.* Newbury Park, CA: Sage.

Johnstone, Barbara. 1990. *Stories, Community, and Place: Narratives from Middle America.* Bloomington: Indiana University Press.

—— 1996. *The Linguistic Individual: Self-Expression in Language and Linguistics.* New York: Oxford University Press.

Johns-Lewis, Catherine (ed.) 1986. *Intonation in Discourse.* Beckenham: Croom Helm.

Julia, Pere. 1983. *Explanatory Models in Linguistics: A Behavioral Perspective.* Princeton, NJ: Princeton University Press.

Kager, René. 1999. *Optimality Theory.* Cambridge: Cambridge University Press.

Kenneally, Christine. 2007. *The First Word: The Search for the Origins of Language.* New York: Viking

Labov, William. 1066. *The Social Stratification of English in New York City.* Washington, DC: Center for Applied linguistics.

—— 1972. *Language in the Inner City: Studies in the Black English Vernacular.* Philadelphia: University of Pennsylvania Press.

—— 1972. *Sociolinguistic Patterns.* University of Pennsylvania Press.

—— 1994. *Principles of Linguistic Change: Volume 1: Internal Factors.* Oxford: Blackwell.

—— 2001. *Principles of Linguistic Change: Volume 2: Social Factors.* Oxford: Blackwell.

Labov, William, Sharon Ash, and Charles Boberg. 2006. *The Atlas of North American English: Phonetics, Phonology and Change.* Berlin: Mouton de Gruyter.

Ladefoged, Peter. 1993. *A Course in Phonetics,* 3rd ed. Forth Worth: Harcourt Brace Jovanovich.

—— 2003. *Phonetic Data Analysis: An Introduction to Fieldwork and Instrumental Techniques.* Oxford: Blackwell.

Ladefoged, Peter and Ian Maddieson. 1996. *The Sounds of the World's Languages.* Oxford: Blackwell.

Lakoff, George and Mark Johnson. 1980. *Metaphors We Live By.* Chicago: University of Chicago Press.

Lakoff, George and Mark Turner. 1989. *More than Cool Reason: A Field Guide to Poetic Metaphor.* Chicago: University of Chicago Press.

Lass, Roger. 1984. *Phonology: An Introduction to Basic Concepts.* Cambridge: Cambridge University Press.

Leech, Geoffrey N. 1969. *A Linguistic Guide to English Poetry.* London: Longman.

Leith, Dick. 1997. *A Social History of English,* 2nd ed. London: Routledge.

Leonard, Tom. 1984. *Intimate Voices: Selected Work 1965–1983.* Newcastle upon Tyne: Galloping Dog Press.

Le Page, R.B. and Andrée Tabouret-Keller. 1985. *Acts of Identity: Creole-based Approaches to Language and Ethnicity.* Cambridge: Cambridge University Press.

Lerner, Gene H. (ed.) 2004. *Conversation Analysis: Studies from the First Generation.* Amsterdam: John Benjamins.

Levinson, Stephen C. 1983. *Pragmatics.* Cambridge: Cambridge University Press.

—— 2000. *Presumptive Meanings: The Theory of Generalized Conversational Implicature.* Cambridge, Mass.: MIT Press.

Lieberman, Philip. 2006. *Toward an Evolutionary Biology of Language.* Cambridge, Mass.: Belknap Press.

Linell, Per. 1998. *Approaching Dialogue: Talk, Interaction and Contexts in Dialogical Perspectives.* Amsterdam: John Benjamins.

——2005. *The Written Language Bias in Linguistics: Its Nature, Origins and Transformations.* London: Routledge.

Lippi-Green, Rosina. 1997. *English with an Accent: Language, Ideology, and Discrimination in the United States.* London: Routledge.

Lyons, John. 1995. *Linguistic Semantics: An Introduction.* Cambridge: Cambridge University Press.

Macaulay, Ronald. 1977. *Language, Social Class, and Education: A Glasgow Study.* Edinburgh: Edinburgh University Press.

—— 1991. *Locating Dialect in Discourse: The Language of Honest Men and Bonnie Lasses in Ayr.* New York: Oxford University Press.

——2005a. *Talk That Counts: Age, Gender, and Social Class Differences in Discourse.* New York: Oxford University Press.

—— 2005b. *Extremely Common Eloquence: Constructing Scottish Identity through Narrative.* Amsterdam: Rodopi.

—— 2006. *The Social Art: Language and Its Uses,* 2nd Ed. New York: Oxford University Press.

Maddieson, Ian. 1984. *Patterns of Sound.* Cambridge: Cambridge University Press.

Mallory, J.P. and D.Q. Adams (eds.) 1997. *Encyclopedia of Indo-European Culture.* London: Fitzroy Dearborn.

Marchal, Alain. 2009. *From Speech Physiology to Linguistic Phonetics.* Hobdon, NJ: Wiley.

Marchand, Hans. 1966. *The Categories and Types of Present-day English Word-formation*. University of Alabama Press.

Matthews, C.M. 1972. *Place-names of the English-speaking World*. New York: Scribner's.

Matthews, P.H. 1979. *Generative Grammar and Linguistic Competence*. London: Allen and Unwin.

—— 1991. *Morphology*. Cambridge: Cambridge University Press.

McCafferty, Kevin. 2001. *Ethnicity and Language Change: English in (London) Derry, Northern Ireland*. Amsterdam: John Benjamins.

McCawley, James D. 1988. *The Syntactic Phenomena of English*, 2 vols. Chicago: University of Chicago Press.

McIntosh, Angus, Michael L. Samuels, and Michael Benskin (eds.) 1986. *A Linguistic Atlas of Late Mediaeval English*, 4 vols. Aberdeen: Aberdeen University Press.

Miller, Jim and Regina Weinert. 1995. *Spontaneous Spoken Language: Syntax and Discourse*. Oxford: Oxford University Press.

Milroy, James. 1992. *Linguistic Variation and Change: On the Historical Sociolinguistics of English*. Oxford: Blackwell.

Milroy, Lesley. *Language and Social Networks*, 2nd ed. Oxford: Blackwell.

Milroy, Lesley and Matthew Gordon. 2003. *Sociolinguistics: Method and Interpretation*. Oxford: Blackwell.

Milroy, Lesley and Pieter Musken (eds.) 1995. *One Speaker, Two Languages: Cross-disciplinary perspectives on code-switching*. Cambridge: Cambridge University Press.

Moerman, Michael. 1988. *Talking Culture: Ethnography and Conversation Analysis*. Philadelphia: University of Pennsylvania Press.

Mufwene, Salikoko. 2001. *The Ecology of Language Evolution*. Cambridge: Cambridge University Press.

Newmeyer, Frederick J. 1986. *Linguistic Theory in America*, 2nd ed. Orlando, FL: Academic Press.

—— 2005. *Possible and Probable Languages: A Generative Perspective on Linguistic Typology*. Oxford: Oxford University Press.

Nicolaisen, W.F.H. 1976. *Scottish Place-Names*. London: Batsford.

Nofsinger, Robert E. 1991. *Everyday Conversation*. Newbury Park: Sage.

Obler, Lorraine and Kris Gjerlow. 1999. *Language and the Brain*. Cambridge: Cambridge University Press.

Ogden, C.K. and I.A.Richards. 1923. *The Meaning of Meaning*.

O'Grady, William. 2005. *Syntactic Carpentry: An Emergent Approach to Syntax*. Mahwah, NJ: Lawrence Erlbaum.

Oppenheimer, Stephen. 2006. *The Origins of the British: A Genetic Detective Story: The Surprising Roots of the English, Irish, Scottish, and Welsh*. New York: Carroll & Graf.

Palmer, Frank R. 1981. *Semantics*. Cambridge: Cambridge University Press.

Pederson, Lee (ed.) 1986. *Linguistic Atlas of the Gulf States*. Athens: University of Georgia Press.

Preston, Dennis R. 1989. *Perceptual Dialectology*, Dordrecht: Foris.1

—— (ed.). 1991. *American Dialect Research*. Amsterdam: John Benjamins.

Preston, Dennis R. (ed.) 2003. *Needed Research in American Dialects*. Durham, NC: Duke University Press. (Publication No. 88 of the American Dialect Society.)

Quirk, Randolph, Sidney Greenbaum, Geoffrey Leech, and Jan Svartvik. 1985. *A Comprehensive Grammar of the English Language*. London: Longman.

Reaney, P.H. 1958. *A Dictionary of British Surnames*. London: Routledge and Kegan Paul.

—— 1967. *The Origin of English Surnames*. London: Routledge and Kegan Paul.

Rickford, John R. 1999. *African American Vernacular English: Features, Evolution, Educational Implications*. Oxford: Blackwell.

Rissanen, MattiMerja Kytő, and Kirsi Heikkonen (eds.) 1997. *English in Transition: Corpus-based Studies in Linguistic Variation and genre Styles*. Berlin: Mouton de Gruyter.

Romaine, Suzanne. 1995. *Bilingualism*. Oxford: Blackwell.

—— 1994. *Language in Society: An Introduction to Sociolinguistics*. Oxford: Oxford University Press.

Room, Adrian. 1988. *Dictionary of Place-names in the British Isles*. London: Bloomsbury.

Sacks, Harvey. 1992. *Lectures on Conversation.*, ed. by Gail Jefferson, 2.vols. Oxford: Blackwell.

Saussure, Ferdinand de. 1922. *Cours de Linguistique Générale*. Paris: Payot.

——1966. *Course in General Linguistics*. (Trans. by Wade Baskin.) New York: McGraw-Hill.

—— 1986. *Course in General Linguistics*. (Trans. by Roy Harris.) La Salle, IL: Open Court.

Schegloff, Emanuel A. 2007. *Sequence Organization in Interaction: A Primer in Conversation Analysis*. Cambridge: Cambridge University Press.

Schiffrin, Deborah. 1987. *Discourse Markers*. Cambridge: Cambridge University Press.

Sells, Peter. 1985. *Lectures on Contemporary Syntactic Theories: An Introduction to Government-Binding Theory, Generalized Phrase Structure Grammar, and Lexical-Functional Grammar*. Stanford: CSLI Publications.

Seuren, Pieter A.M. 2004. *Chomsky's Minimalism.* New York: Oxford University Press.

Smith, Elsdon. C. 1969. *American Surnames.* Philadelphia: Chilton.

Smith, Jeremy. 1996. *An Historical Study of English: Function, Form and Change.* London: Routledge.

Smith, Neil. 1999. *Chomsky: Ideas and Ideals.* Cambridge: Cambridge University Press.

Snyder, William. 2007. *Child Language: The Parametric Approach.* Oxford: Oxford University Press.

Spencer, Andrew. 1991. *An Introduction to Word Structure in Generative Grammar.* Oxford: Blackwell.

Stemmer, Brigitte and Harry A. Whitaker (eds.) 1998. *Handbook of Neurolinguistics.* San Diego: Academic Press.

Tagliamonte, Sali A. 2006. *Analyzing Sociolinguistic Variation.* Cambridge: Cambridge University Press.

Tannen, Deborah. 2005. *Conversational Style: Analyzing Talk among Friends ,*2ⁿᵈ ed. New York: Oxford University Press.

Trousdale, Graeme and Nikolas Gisborne (eds.) 2008. *Topics in English Linguistics: Constructional Approaches to English Grammar.* Berlin: Mouton de Gruyter.

Trudgill, Peter. 1974. *The Social Differentiation of English in Norwich.* Cambridge: Cambridge University Press.

—— 2001. *Sociolinguistics: An Introduction.* 4th ed. Baltimore: Penguin.

Urciuoli, Bonnie. 1996. *Exposing Prejudice: Puerto Rican Experiences of Language, Race, and Class.* Boulder, CO: Westview Press.

Williams, Raymond. 1988. *Keywords: A Vocabulary of Culture and Society.* London: Fontana.

Wolfram, Walt. 1969. *A Sociolinguistic Description of Detroit Negro Speech.* Washington, DC: Center for Applied Linguistics.

Wolfram, Walt and Natalie Schilling-Estes. 1998. *American English: Dialects and Variation.* Oxford: Blackwell.

# Index

198 *Index*